Our Haunted
Planet

Our Haunted Planet

John A. Keel

1999
Galde Press, Inc.
Lakeville, Minnesota, U.S.A.

First Galde Press Edition, 1999
First Printing, 1999
Previously published by Fawcett Publications, Inc., 1971

Cover design by David F. Godwin

Portions of chapters 14 and 15 appeared originally in *Saga* magazine, copyright 1968
and 1970 by Gambi Publications, Inc.; and in *Male* magazine, copyright 1970 by
Magazine Management, Inc. Chapter 16 is excerpted from lectures delivered by the
author before the Humanist Society, July 22, 1970, and the American Society of
Dowsers, October 2, 1970.

ISBN 1–880090–16–3

Galde Press, Inc.
PO Box 460
Lakeville, Minnesota 55044–0460

Thank you, Mr. Apol, wherever you are.

Publisher's Note

Thought by some to be John Keel's best work, this book offers a comprehensive survey of unexplained phenomena on our haunted planet. It represents a detached, objective, and intelligent overview by a well-known working investigator. *Our Haunted Planet* was originally published in 1971. Consequently, some of the material may seem dated—particularly the final chapter (now cast in the past tense), which, with the advantage of hindsight, seems terribly overoptimistic about the hippie phenomenon. Some individuals no longer among the living are referred to as if alive and in business, although in some cases this information has been updated. There are also a number of statements that, to our more enlightened generation, may seem to be somewhat politically incorrect. We apologize to any who may be offended.

Contents

Introduction

IN SEPTEMBER 1953, I spent eight hours inside the Great Pyramid in Egypt producing a radio program that was aired throughout Europe over the American Forces Network (AFN) the following month. Egypt so impressed me, and archaeology so fascinated me, that I returned to Cairo the next year and lived there for several months, wading through the musty libraries and museums, prowling the desert, and visiting the ancient tombs. During a trek to Aswan and the Upper Nile, I saw my first flying saucer, a metallic looking disk, with a rotating outer rim, which hovered for several minutes above the Aswan Dam in broad daylight. I had written and produced a radio documentary, *Things in the Sky*, in 1952, and my earlier researches into unidentified flying objects had already convinced me that such things not only existed, but that they had been present in our skies since the dawn of man.

Eventually my travels took me to Beirut, Damascus, Baghdad, and a thousand places in between. I walked among the ancient ruins and puzzled over man's illustrious but forgotten past. In India I wandered alone into the Himalayas and crossed the border of Tibet (which has since been sealed by the Chinese). As I traveled, I interviewed archaeologists, historians, and assorted experts and spent endless hours in remote libraries poring over rare old books. I was puzzled at first to discover that none of the leading authorities seemed to agree on anything. Indeed, a large part of the scientific literature is devoted to theorization and incredibly vicious attacks on the theories of other theorists. Most perplexing of all was the fact that some of the literature about the ruins I had visited smacked of pure fiction, because the authors had not visited the sites but labored instead to couple fictitious theories with dubious facts. This led, of course, to conclusions that bordered on the imbecilic.

An offshoot of this process is, understandably enough, an enormous quantity of crank literature created by unqualified researchers who attempted to interpret the scientific material in their own ways. In many areas of the less popular sciences the crank material outweighs the scientific because few if any scientists have tackled those subjects. So ninety-eight percent of all the available literature on Atlantis, flying saucers, Tibet, and prehistoric ruins falls into the crank category. The task of sorting all this out and developing a valid synthesis is a formidable one—one that I have undertaken with great trepidation.

In his book, *In the Name of Science,* Martin Gardner defines the characteristics of the common crank or pseudoscientist. He lists the four chief attributes as being: (1) The crank considers himself a genius...even a towering genius who is years ahead of his time. (2) He considers his colleagues and fellow researchers "ignorant blockheads," largely because they fail to recognize his genius. He assaults his opponents by impugnation, questioning their honesty, intelligence, and motives. They respond in kind, naturally, and so great storms are whipped up in the trivial teacups of the scientific and pseudoscientific journals. Controversy is the lifeblood of crankism. (3) The pseudoscientist is paranoid and feels he is the victim of a vast conspiracy designed to suppress his brilliant work. In many instances these imagined conspiracies become a vital part of the subject itself, as for example, the endless literature discussing how the U.S. Air Force has been keeping the truth about flying saucers from the public. (4) The crank delights in focusing his attacks "on the greatest scientists and the best-established theories." He goes after big game. He is wiser than Einstein, knows more about astronomy than Fred Hoyle, and is better informed about the moon than Neil Armstrong.

The crank also invents his own terminology: a jabberwocky understood only by him and his closest allies. So we find the literature filled with confusing and complicated terms that are merely displays of pseudoerudition, or what psychiatrists call neologisms.

Over the years I have met the leaders of many peculiar cults and pseudo-scientific factions of belief. With very few exceptions, they have all lived up to the above criteria. Most were friendly and cooperative with me until they realized that I did not share their beliefs in Atlantis or visitors from Androm-eda. Then they turned on me with wrathful vengeance and launched such campaigns of unfounded slander that I could only be amazed and amused. I have now been accused of being everything from a Communist con man to a secret agent for the Central Intelligence Agency; from a religious fanatic (I'm a lifelong agnostic) to a pawn of the devil. Typographical errors, over which I have no control, in my many articles and books have been lovingly dissected by these groups and prompted countless letters and essays review-ing their sinister implications. After twenty-five years as a writer and reporter dedicated to collecting the facts as objectively and as honestly as possible, my integrity has been attacked from all angles.

For these reasons this book is written in a style that discusses known facts with the popular and unpopular beliefs they have inspired. I am not supporting *any* of these beliefs. I am merely discussing them. It may be that the great civilizations of Atlantis and Lemuria once actually flourished on this planet. In this book I am only weighing the evidence pro and con. It may be that little green men from Mars really are visiting housewives in Nebraska. I am only reporting the claims of the housewives, not trying to prove that Martians are really dropping in. The believers in Atlantis will undoubtedly hate me. The believers in Martians already despise me.

Parts of this book are so obviously tongue-in-cheek that it shouldn't be necessary to mention it. Yet I know from bitter experience that some of my humorous comments will be taken seriously and will prompt new venom. I am not attacking any specific individuals or cults. I am attacking man's abysmal ignorance and his impassioned effort to hide that ignorance from himself. I have seen a large part of this world and its mysteries. Wonder and curiosity have always been an integral part of my life. I am only trying to share that wonder with the reader.

This book is based upon countless interviews, endless correspondence, many in-depth personal investigations, and hundreds of books covering everything from alchemy to zoology. Wherever possible, I have tried to include key source references for the benefit of those readers who might be interested in pursuing some of these matters further. It has been impossible, however, to list all my sources. Some of the books used in my research were privately published and are quite rare.

Although unidentified flying objects are mentioned frequently in these pages, the UFO controversy is not the main theme. Some of the major UFO cases discussed are drawn from reports that appeared originally in England's *Flying Saucer Review*, the only truly scientific publication devoted to the subject. Queries should be directed to Flying Saucer Review, FSR Publications, Ltd., PO Box 162, High Wycombe, Bucks HP13 5DZ, England.

I do not pretend to know any answers. After a lifetime of travel and study I am still learning the questions. This is a journey into man's past and the curious manifestations that have always surrounded him and that have directed the human race upward from the caves to the moon itself. It is a journey into a jungle of myth, legend, and belief, and hopefully, it is another small step toward the larger truth that man has always sought but never really found.

—JOHN A. KEEL

Part One

Archaeology is not a science, it's a vendetta.
—Sir Mortimer Wheeler

Chapter One

"You can't get there from here."

WHILE HAIRY, BEETLED-BROWED cavemen were laboring to invent fire and the wheel, there already existed on this planet a highly developed civilization of intelligent beings. They built massive cities of stone, many of which are still standing. They methodically constructed giant mounds of earth all over this planet for some purpose that still escapes us. They scattered peculiar artifacts of stone and metal across every continent, and they sailed every ocean, mapping the entire globe systematically.

Then they vanished.

Cavemen inherited the earth. They regarded the ancient cities as sacred places. As the centuries ticked off, they became conscious of other life forms around them. Life forms that seemed to possess the power of invisibility, of life and death itself. They invented names for these forms. They worshiped them. They recorded the manifestations of that invisible world in myths and legends handed down from generation to generation. Eventually they perfected sciences based upon their observations of those manifestations. In time those sciences developed new myths. The original owners of the earth, the builders of those great cities, were forgotten. But as men spread across the face of the planet, the traces of those lost Elders were rediscovered. Man's newfangled sciences couldn't fit such traces into their new concepts, however, so the evidence was ignored. As a result, the earth has two histories: the history taught in our colleges and schools, and the real but ignored history of a very ancient people and of strange forces that have often supervised human events.

Ten thousand years ago that unknown civilization carefully mapped the entire surface of the globe. Their maps were copied and recopied and passed along from one age to the next. Finally, copies of them were rediscovered by Capt. Arlington H. Mallery in, of all places, the Library of Congress. Known as the *Piri Re'is* maps, they were originally found among the relics in the former imperial palace of the Sultan of Constantinople in 1929. Eventually they ended up in the archives in Washington, D.C. At first glance these maps, which are dated A.D. 1513, appear to be nothing more than a hopelessly garbled view of the ancient world. No one paid much attention to them until Captain Mallery came along. Working with the U.S. Hydrographic Office and the Weston Observatory of Boston, he developed a grid system that suddenly brought the maps into focus. The modern Mercator grid system was not invented until 1559, so the ancient surveyors had to develop a method of their own. Once Mallery had unscrambled that method, he could hardly believe the results.

These maps were incredibly detailed and as accurate as the latest charts. Antarctica, for example, was not discovered until Captain Cook reached it in 1773, and it was not fully explored until the 1950s. But the frozen continent is laid out with almost pinpoint accuracy on the *Piri Re'is* maps, including mountain ranges that were not even known to us until 1952!

Even more astonishing, these maps outline glaciers and land areas that are known to have existed in the Ice Age...before the last great shift of the earth's crust an estimated ten thousand years ago. This fact led Mallery to conclude that the original on which the *Piri Re'is* maps were apparently based had to have been drawn before the Ice Age.

Professor Charles Hapgood, a science historian, heard of Mallery's work and turned the maps into a class study project at Keene State College. His students painstakingly compared each detail with modern charts and found that the ancient maps were never more than five degrees off...and those errors were probably due to land movements that occurred after the originals were drawn. Many of the details on the early maps correlated precisely with modern surveys. The results of Hapgood's studies, together with full-color reproductions of the maps, were published in a book titled *Maps of the Ancient Sea Kings.*

Modern scientists can't seem to agree on the age of mankind. Each year produces a new bit of bone and a new controversy. Some claim man might be half a million years old. Others offer more conservative estimates ranging between thirty to seventy thousand years. But all seem to share the notion that our ancestors were embarrassingly primitive ten thousand years ago. They certainly were not developed enough to sail and chart the earth.

It would have been impossible for anyone to contrive the maps in 1929, the year they were found in Constantinople. It would have been even more impossible for someone to hoax them in 1513. And it is downright ridiculous to think that someone could have surveyed the earth before the Ice Age. Modern scientists have a very scientific method for coping with such humiliating discoveries. They put them in the basements of their museums and forget about them.

The museums are filled with such erratics, as they are called. A cube of metal, carefully machined, notched, and rounded on one side, was found in the center of a block of coal in Austria in 1885. It's still in a museum in Salzburg and no one has ever come up with an explanation for it. Basing their conclusions on the age of the coal bed, various experts have estimated it to be three hundred thousand years old. That makes it quite a bit younger than the piece of gold thread that workmen found imbedded in eight feet of rock at a quarry in Rutherford Mills, England. The London *Times* announced the discovery on June 22, 1844…and the experts mumbled that it had to be sixty million years old. Who could have dropped a gold thread in England sixty million years ago? Or who could have manufactured that iron and nickel cube three hundred thousand years back? Maybe these things were the handiwork of the same people who made the strange pieces of very ancient pottery that have been found in rock quarries and coal mines around the world along with steel nails, perfect glass lenses, and even—believe it or not—bones of prehistoric animals with bullets in them. Giant chains have been found imbedded in great rocks in both North and South America. Not merely imbedded but actually passing through the rocks. They seem to predate the arrival of the Europeans by thousands of years.

Electric batteries have been found in ancient Egyptian tombs. A huge slab of perfect green glass weighing many tons was found in a cave in Israel a few years ago. It ranks as the largest piece of glass ever cast and is very ancient. Who made it, how, and why are still unsolved mysteries.

Science tells us one thing: these artifacts put the lie to all the scientific theories. Take man's earliest records—the cave paintings. Scientists assert that the great saurians were extinct long before man arrived on the scene. Yet cave paintings have been found depicting dinosaurs. Other cliff carvings in the Southwest show men hurling weapons at gigantic creatures that look like elephants or mammoths.

Captain Mallery created a stir when he first revealed his work with the *Piri Re'is* maps on a broadcast from Georgetown University in 1956. He dared to suggest that the maps may have been the product of an *aerial survey*. Professor Hapgood was more cautious, however, and merely implied they were the work of some lost seafaring culture. The aerial survey hypothesis would have necessarily been dependent upon a highly advanced technological society. Not only would flying machines have been required, but photography would also be needed for such a survey. Did the Elders have cameras, too?

A mere forty-seven thousand years ago somebody carved an intriguing picture on the side of the Hunan Mountains in China. A picture of cylinders in the sky with strange beings standing on them. Russian and Chinese archaeologists could date it, but they couldn't explain it. Nor could they explain the drawing they found carved in a cliff at Fergana in Central Asia in 1961. A *Reuters* dispatch described it as resembling a man wearing an "airtight helmet" with some kind of mechanical contraption on his back. It has been dated at 7000 B.C. Other peculiar cave and cliff carvings have been found in South America, Japan, and the Sahara Desert. Some of these pictures show giants with round heads towering over ordinary hunters. Others depict circular objects with odd creatures coming out of them. These drawings were apparent attempts to record highly unusual and significant events, but today they are open to all kinds of interpretation and speculation.

Scattered throughout France are many ancient caverns heavily decorated with carvings and paintings dating back ten to thirty thousand years. More than two thousand animals are depicted, including 610 horses, 510 bison, 205 mammoths, and 176 ibex, according to a study published by R. Breuil in 1952. Alongside this impressive menagerie there are scores of other designs that are far more mysterious. They show oval- and disk-shaped objects, some apparently standing on tripod legs with ladders extending down from them. Archaeologists can't account for them, but they look uneasily like the modern descriptions of flying saucers. The leading French authority, Aimé Michel, goes so far as to suggest that that is exactly what they are.

Ancient records in China describe flying saucers and mysterious lights in the sky. They were usually regarded as dragons, and the early Chinese noted that these things flew regular routes year after year, century after century. Other early manuscripts preserved in India mention *vimanas,* "aerial cars," as if they were commonplace. Five thousand years ago a sage named Maharishi Bharadwaj wrote a thorough description of these *vimanas,* telling how they could move in all directions silently, cover vast distances, and even become invisible. They were supposedly propelled by "tunes and rhythms"…perhaps a poetic way of describing the humming and whirring of intricate and little-understood machinery. In appearance they resembled the flying cones that have been frequently described in the reports of modern UFO witnesses around the globe.

Although this sort of evidence is superabundant, it has never been systematically studied by trained scholars. Instead, this material has fallen into the hands of assorted cultists and students of fringe pseudosciences. It has been used to advance belief in everything from lost Atlantis to extraterrestrial visitants from some distant planet. To subscribe to any one of these multitudinous beliefs is to exclude all other possibilities. We should consider every possibility, avoid belief, and accept only the hard facts.

Two key facts are already clear: (1) There have always been strange objects in the skies above this planet. They were seen by early man and have been seen constantly ever since, as the Bible and other available records still firmly attest. (2) Somebody mapped the earth before the Ice Age. We have no way of knowing who they were or how they did it. If the *Piri Re'is* maps were the product of an aerial survey, then perhaps there *was* an advanced civilization somewhere in the Americas or the Pacific, removed from the random clusters of primitive men. But occasionally the advanced culture dropped in on the cave men or at least flew overhead. Thus two cultures may have existed simultaneously. One highly advanced and purposely aloof from the other—the animal-like cave dwellers. It was inevitable that the two cultures should occasionally cross and that the higher group should affect the lower in many ways. At some point in early history the higher culture was either destroyed by a monumental catastrophe or withdrew in some fashion, leaving hardly a trace behind. So our entire record of that superculture comes from the observations of primitive man. Our only evidence is the flimsy overlapping that took place: the residue of the effect of the superculture upon the subculture.

Primitive man was profoundly influenced by the superculture and guided by it. There are even indications that members of the superculture actually appeared before primitive man and took over as kings and god-kings to direct his early development. Such appearances helped to generate many of man's first religious beliefs.

Some 2,500,000 people believe in the *Book of Mormon,* the Mormon bible, which is purportedly a record of life in North America thousands of years ago. As with all such records from all cultures and all religions, there are frequent descriptions of events in which some unknown benevolent group supplied man with direct help in an hour of need. For example, here is how a compass was introduced, presumably, to those long forgotten North Americans:

> And it came to pass that as my father arose in the morning and went forth to the tent door, to his great astonishment he beheld upon the ground a round ball of curious workmanship; and it was of fine brass. And within the ball were two spindles; and the one pointed the way whither we should go into the wilderness. (I Nephi 16:10)

One of the most popular theories bandied about in cultist circles is that man was seeded on this planet by some interplanetary group and that this group has kindy, but remotely, observed and guided our progress ever since. If this were true, they have been doing a lousy job in recent centuries. We need a lot more help than they have been giving us.

In H. G. Wells' prophetic *Things to Come* there is a vision of a world ravaged by war and divided into fierce tribes ruled by warlords. A handful of surviving scientists and thinkers band together and begin the task of restoring civilization by flying over the planet. They call their organization Wings over the World (WOW). Much of the UFO evidence suggests that a real WOW has always existed. Maybe one of their members handed a cave man the first flaming brand and the first wheel, just as some unknown party allegedly deposited the first compass outside that Mormon tent.

A friend from WOW could have handed the original *Piri Re'is* map to some ancient Egyptian. After him it may have passed from the library at Alexandria to the palace in Constantinople. The key to the grid system was lost, so the map became useless. However, it is known that Christopher Columbus did have some strange maps when he set out for his shortcut to India.*

It is easy to speculate and even easier to leap to mind-blowing conclusions. We must try instead to assemble the many fragments of tantalizing evidence and attempt to construct the whole. To do this, we must first recognize some very unpleasant facts. We must admit just how stupid we really are.

Several different scientists attached to the National Aeronautics and Space Administration (NASA) have issued humble public statements admitting that our space program has produced data that invalidates many of the most coveted conclusions and beliefs of our learned astronomers. Ideas that have been accepted as fact for many years have suddenly been proved completely false. The more we find out about the moon, the less we know about it. Space probes to Mars and Venus have tossed innumerable astronomical theories into a cocked hat. Radar probes to the planet Mercury discovered that the planet is actually rotating slowly on its axis, even though millions

---

*See Arlington H. Mallery. *Lost America.*

of schoolchildren have been taught for generations that Mercury does *not* rotate. Leading astronomers are now arguing over the status of Jupiter. Some now suspect that it isn't a planet at all but is really a cold star.

For the past two centuries, astronomers have been peering through telescopes, counting stars, and making mathematical calculations to account for the motions and flickerings they have observed. They have published and taught their learned conclusions as the gospel. Now we know that they have been wrong in many key areas. Before long, all the textbooks will have to be scrapped. All of the old ideas will be discarded.

"We used to think of the universe as nothing more than abundant fields of stars arranged in galaxies," Dr. Frank Drake, chairman of Cornell University's astronomy department, said recently. "But we underestimated the variety and quantity of matter in space by a factor of about one trillion. Which means that we were about as wrong as we could be."

In the early 1960s deep-dished radio telescopes discovered a maze of radio signals pouring in from outer space. At first there were wild speculations that we had made contact with some supercivilization in some other galaxy. But further study discounted this fascinating notion. Instead, it was found that interstellar space is filled with invisible objects that don't emit light rays but that do give off powerful radio waves. These things have been dubbed quasars and pulsars. They constitute one rather trivial aspect of a broad and complex phenomenon. Our haunted planet has always been bathed in mysterious electromagnetic propagation and radio waves, *some of them intelligent signals* of unknown origin. We have been aware of these signals ever since the invention of the radio receiver, but we still can't account for them. All of this will be discussed in depth in another chapter.

Just as those funny flying saucers seem to be an environmental mystery that has always existed on this planet, it also seems that the earth's atmosphere has always been charged with unidentified radio signals—some of which seem to radiate from the planet itself…as if the earth were beaming signals into space in response to the signals being received. Of course, the cultists contend that WOW has established secret transmitters in underground caverns.

Even gravity is a mystery. Newton discovered the hard way that if you sit under an apple tree, you are apt to get hit on the head by a falling apple. But we still don't know why. Recent experiments indicate that gravity is really a slowly pulsing wave pouring across space, beating about once per hour. The source of this wave and its true nature are a puzzle. We thought we knew something about it until our astronauts went into space and fumbled around in weightlessness. They found that even friction disappears in space.

R. Buckminster Fuller, the great thinker and designer, said, "Everything you've learned in school as 'obvious' becomes less and less obvious as you begin to study the universe. For example, there are no solids in the universe. There's not even a suggestion of a solid. There are no absolute continuums. There are no surfaces. There are no straight lines."

Everything is up for grabs. We don't know anything about the universe or outer space. We have in all likelihood constructed a totally false history of our own race. And most humiliating of all, although we have lived on this planet for at least forty thousand years, we really don't know much about it. Worse still, we haven't even explored it!

Vast sections of this planet encompassing hundreds of thousands of square miles have never been surveyed. There are enormous regions that still have not been visited by a single scientifically trained man. Seasoned travelers are wearily familiar with the problem of locating accurate maps. In many countries in Africa, Asia, and South America detailed maps are simply unobtainable because no surveys have ever been made. Those maps which are available often have the rivers and mountains in the wrong places. Here in the United States precisely detailed maps of many areas just don't exist. There are blank spots in Maine and even in New Jersey. The average road map doled out by service stations includes only the major highways and the larger towns. Unincorporated villages—and they number in the thousands—can't be found on any map anywhere. The regional maps distributed by the Geological Survey in Washington are often based upon surveys made in 1880 or 1920, so many of them are virtually useless. New highways are being built so rapidly that the average road map is two to five years behind.

Travelers to inland Brazil find themselves trying to cope with maps based on sketches drawn by missionaries a hundred years ago. Visitors to the Himalaya Mountains have to deal with maps drawn by amateur cartographers and guesswork. Vast sections of the earth's oceans have not been adequately charted. There are countless islands everywhere that have never been visited, named, or mapped. If WOW actually exists, they could occupy a large island in the Pacific or Antarctica and nobody would ever be the wiser.

We have, of course, flown over a great part of the earth. Back in the 1930s Charles Lindbergh flew over Brazil and reported seeing an enormous stone wall deep in the jungle. A wall that stretched for miles. No explorer has ever penetrated to that wall overland. We still don't know anything about it. Other fliers in other parts of the world have reported similar oddities and most of them remain unexplored mysteries.

In 1970 the United Nations issued a report that stated that four-fifths of the earth's surface was inadequately surveyed and charted and that tremendous areas remain unexplored altogether. The cartographers who drew up the original *Piri Re'is* maps probably knew more about our planet than we do.

Despite all these facts, most of us like to pretend that our planet is fully explored and that all of its many mysteries have been adequately solved. We believe our history books. In fact, many millions of people still cling to the thoroughly discredited religious belief that mankind is only four thousand years old. Science labors to ignore the mounting evidence that we may not be the only intelligent life form on this planet. Yet historians have always carefully recorded the events that indicate that a parahuman race does exist alongside us. Millions of people have encountered them and thousands of books have been written about those encounters.

Now that we are zooming headlong into the Age of Aquarius, it is time for us to take a new look at the world around us; time for us to study those despicable erratics of archaeology and history; time for us to think about the unthinkable. Our much-touted technology has led us down the road to ruin, poisoned our environment, and given us the implements for destroying the earth itself. If there was a great superculture thousands of years ago, perhaps it followed the same tragic course. Perhaps even the Abominable Snowmen of the Himalayas and their North American counterparts, the Sasquatch of Canada, will inherit the earth, and ten thousand years from now their descendants will be studying a frayed copy of an old road map and speculating about us. Naturally, there will be scientists among them who will sneer at the whole thing...and then they will get back to the business of trying to split the atom.

Chapter Two

The Continent That Vanished

EVERY TWO OR THREE YEARS some adventurous scientist or peripatetic deep-sea diver discovers lost Atlantis. He usually announces his find during the summer silly season when news is slow, and the papers are filled with yarns about the Loch Ness monster and bathing beauty contests. Atlantis has now been located in the Mediterranean (many times), west of the Azores, south of the Azores, in the Caribbean, off the west coast of South America, off the east coast of South America, in the North Pacific, in the South Pacific, off the coast of Florida, and even in the Indian Ocean.

Recently the ruins of an ancient temple of unknown origin were discovered in the blue waters off the Bahamas. The newspapers soberly revealed that Atlantis had been found at last. A year or so later a mysterious stone pillar was spotted by divers deep in the ocean off the coast of Peru. Atlantis rose again.

This game has been going on for a very long time. Researchers wading through fifty-year-old newspapers have found them sprinkled with wondrous tales of Atlantean finds. Professors and Ph.D.s have frequently joined the clamor, bidding for publicity (and the often sizable foundation grants that follow such publicity), keeping alive one of the great fantasies of human history. It isn't even a myth or legend; there isn't enough evidence of any kind to give Atlantis such stature. Nevertheless, Atlantis has become an important part of our folklore. Even the famous prophet Edgar Cayce discussed the lost continent with the spirit world and passed along the prediction that it would rise again in the stormy Atlantic in 1968–69.

While the reality of Atlantis can be viewed with considerable skepticism, the persistence of the belief in it provides some interesting facts about the weird mechanisms employed by the earth's phantom inhabitants to generate myths and camouflage their real existence. Atlantis is no more real than visitors from Mars. Yet there are millions of people who have believed wholeheartedly in both. The members of WOW have carefully sowed the seeds of such myths in their wake and have worked across the generations to nurture them.

First, how did the story of Atlantis begin? It was launched by a single man named Plato (427–347 B.C.). In his two dialogues *Timaeus* and *Critias*, he offers a description of Atlantis and its demise *nine thousand years* earlier. His source, he states, is a man named Critias, who had heard the story from his great-grandfather Dropides, who had heard it from a sage named Solon, who had heard it from an Egyptian priest. So the whole foundation of the Atlantis fantasy is based upon what a ninety-year-old man told a ten-year-old boy (those are the ages given by Plato) about a tale spun by Solon years before. Rather like having your own great-grandfather tell you the plot of a novel that someone else described to him after having heard it from someone else in a far-off land. And that someone else hadn't read the novel but had only heard about it, since the novel was nine thousand years old.

Incidentally, the final pages of Plato's discourse are missing, so even his record of this hearsay is incomplete.

Scholars have devoted their lives to pondering Plato and searching for archaeological evidence to support the existence of Atlantis. Visit any library and you will find shelves of books on the subject. New pro-Atlantis volumes appear each year. A small, indefatigable cult of Atlantean believers has existed for a century or more, pouncing upon each new archaeological discovery as proof of Atlantis. Ruins throughout Central and South America have been credited to the Atlantis culture. Everything from Stonehenge in England to the Great Pyramid in Egypt to the monasteries in the Himalayas has been accepted by the believers as further evidence of Atlantis.

In chapter 1 the premise was stated that mankind could be an offshoot of some earlier superculture. The Atlantophiles have recognized this partially and think of Atlantis as that superculture. The psychic world has supported this contention for years by passing along endless messages about the past glories of Atlantis through mediums, Ouija boards, and the like. Many of these messages have served as the basis for some of the peculiar books that have appeared. Surprisingly, some of the data in this torrent of gibberish can be authenticated historically, but a pattern is hard to establish.

There are people around the world who claim to have actually met the Atlanteans themselves! These percipients (witnesses) describe stately men and women dressed in colorful robes and headdresses, who appear suddenly like ghosts or apparitions. People who have never given Atlantis any thought at all are suddenly confronted by these entities. Such visits can last for hours, according to the percipients. The Atlantean takes great pains to describe the history of Atlantis in detail and when the witness scurries to a library, he or she finds some of the things mentioned in the literature. Eventually the percipient may write a book or pamphlet himself, combining what he has read with what he has been told by the entity. His work is entered into the literature and quoted again and again in new books written by others.

This same phenomenon occurs constantly in religion, spiritualism, and ufodom. In the latter, the entities claim to represent some other planet and they pass along convincing (to the percipient) descriptions of life on other worlds. Like the Atlantean entities, the UFO pilots share their disturbing ability to appear and disappear in thin air. The tall, bearded Atlanteans with their high cheekbones and Oriental eyes are undoubtedly close brethren of the picturesque spacemen, who, incidentally, are most often described the same way.

In occult lore these entities have been described for centuries and are called elementals. The phenomenon takes many forms and undoubtedly inspired the massive folklore on fairies and leprechauns, vampires and demons, and the multitude of ghouls, goblins, and banshees who have always occupied our haunted planet. They appear to have the ability to assume any shape or disguise. Some, if not all, seem to be the product of some complicated hallucinatory process that is able to feed false images into the minds of the percipients. Thus a group of people in a room can sometimes come up with contradictory descriptions of an apparition. Some of the people might not see it at all.

There are, of course, all kinds of psychological factors that could explain some of these hallucinations and apparitions, too. But it is quite remarkable that some of the messages passed along by our elusive Atlanteans are identical to messages passed along to unrelated witnesses who have chatted with spacemen from Ganymede (a satellite of Jupiter). The same mechanism, be it psychic or psychological, is clearly at work in all these cases.

The phenomenon utilizes many other frames of reference. An apparition might pose as an ancient Greek philosopher or as Abraham Lincoln or a deceased pope. There are cases of all these. The folklore of all cultures also takes into account apparitions that pose as exact duplicates of living persons. In Germany such entities have long been known as *dopplegängers.*

The manifestations have also led to the creation of many minor cults, such as the believers in Lemuria (which is supposed to be another lost continent) and Mu. Here again, we find that a large part of the literature is based upon the alleged experiences of those who have encountered Lemurians. In the Middle Ages many people insisted they had visited the underground palaces of the fairies, and volumes were written about the secret commonwealth of the Little People. In modern times the Dero (detrimental robots) myth has blown up around the stories of people who claim they have been taken to the secret caverns occupied by the ancient, secret Dero culture.

In 1944, *Amazing Stories,* a science fiction magazine, published Richard Shaver's "I Remember Lemuria." Editor Ray Palmer was amazed when he was swamped by thousands of letters from people who swore they had had experiences with Deros and Lemurians. They often described things identical to the flying saucer phenomenon (which did not explode on the American scene until 1947).

The myth-making machinery of WOW has always been in operation and the earliest thinkers and scientists recognized it. Strange illusions and purposeful distortions of reality have always haunted the human race. Some cults have defined the culprits as Masters of Illusion, the Black Mentalists, and the X Group. For centuries it was popular to accuse the devil, witches, and warlocks for these bewildering manifestations. Whole religions sprang up around the evidence supplied by the phenomenon.

In Sweden the great mathematician Emanuel Swedenborg (1688–1772) wrote huge tomes about his experiences with the elementals and offered solemn warnings such as:

> When spirits begin to speak with a man, he must beware that he believe nothing that they say. For nearly everything they say is fabricated by them, and they lie: for if they are permitted to narrate anything, as what heaven is and how things in the heavens are to be understood, they would tell so many lies that a man would be astonished. This they would do with solemn affirmation…Wherefore men must beware and not believe them…

Sir Walter Scott (1771–1832), the famous novelist, made a serious study of these matters, and in 1830 he published a series of essays summarizing his conclusions. He noted that when trained psychics encountered fairies and visited their splendid palaces, "the illusion vanished." He explained:

> The young knights and beautiful ladies showed themselves as wrinkled carles and odious hags.…The stately halls were turned into miserable damp caverns—all the delights of the Elfin Elysium vanished at once. In a word, their pleasures were showy but totally unsubstantial—their activity unceasing, but fruitless and unavailing—and their condemnation appears to have consisted in the necessity of maintaining the appearance of industry or enjoyment, though their toil was fruitless and their pleasures shadowy and unsubstantial. Hence poets have designed them as '*the crew that never rest.*' Besides the unceasing and useless bustle in which these spirits seemed to live, they had propensities unfavourable and distressing to mortals.

Educated theologians and scholars attached to the Vatican made a sober investigation into the burgeoning fad of spiritualism in the 1850s. This examination lead to the issuance of a papal bull that warned Catholics that spiritualism was dangerous and the "work of the devil."

Despite all these warnings, millions of people were gripped in the hopeful effort to communicate with the spirit world, and the elementals played the game with relish, implanting a whole new lore about life on other worlds or planes. New cults were spawned and dozens of frames of references were established, all based entirely on the seemingly sincere messages of these characters.

We were guided from beliefs in fairies and their secret commonwealth to new, more scientific beliefs in interplanetary visitors and their great Intergalactic Councils. The flying saucer phenomenon generated a whole new set of theories and beliefs as more and more people had encounters with Venusians and Martians in the back hills of Kentucky and the deserts of Arizona. "The crew that never rest" were up to their old tricks in a new guise.

Once the skilled investigator recognizes just how intangible the manifestations really are, he is catapulted into the more esoteric world of philosophy. He struggles with the task of interpreting these unreal events, trying to understand their hidden purposes. This is unfortunately the route to madness. The phenomenon is fond of creating allegorical situations that cannot be interpreted without excessive scholarship. The problem is to sort out the meaningful from the rubbish and to search for the hidden consistencies buried in the mountains of communications from the past and present.

The scriptures of all the great religions do contain a number of subtle correlations. Much of this literature deals vaguely with rumors of some great past civilization. Isolated Indian tribes in North and South America have legends and myths very similar to the stories found in the Bible, including tales of a great deluge that destroyed most of mankind thousands of years ago. The Toltec Indians, for example, even had a tradition about a *zacuali,* a very high tower they erected, and according to Ixtilxochitl, "Presently their languages were confused, and, not being able to understand each other, they went to different parts of the earth."

Atlantean scholars have labored to assemble all this lore as further proof that Atlantis did indeed exist as a real continent, which was destroyed by some great natural catastrophe. However, much of the information passed along by the Atlantean elementals states that Atlantis was an evil place, dominated by a warlike technology very similar to our own, and that the Atlanteans eventually destroyed themselves—or were deliberately destroyed by some greater force that took a dim view of their militarism.

In flying saucer lore we have tales passed on by the spacemen of a great planet located between Mars and Jupiter and identified variously as Maldek, Clarion, and a dozen other names. The inhabitants of this planet learned to smash the atom and soon succeeded in smashing their entire planet. It was broken into thousands of bits and pieces, and those fragments now constitute the asteroid belt.

So one important thread runs through all this literature: a great civilization once existed prior to the appearance of modern man, and it was either destroyed or destroyed itself. The surviving physical evidence, which will be discussed further on, indicates that such a civilization did exist on this planet and that its inhabitants vanished before, or soon after, man crawled out of his caves.

It may be that the elementals are actually a part of the human psyche and that they have been presenting us with some scrambled racial memory of the distant past. Like the Garden of Eden, Atlantis may be nothing more than an allegory designed to give us a clue about our own history. In flying saucer lore there is elaborately detailed literature asserting that Venus was actually the Garden of Eden and that Adam and Eve were Venusians planted here to colonize earth. Another variation on the Noah's Ark theme.

Even more interesting are the contiguous activities of the parahuman group that has remained in constant touch with us throughout history and has greatly influenced our theological and philosophical ideas. They are proven liars and mischief makers, but it is also possible that they have been slyly trying to tell us something about ourselves. In recent years the flying saucer occupants have passed along innumerable warnings about how we have been upsetting the balance of the universe with our atom bombs. They have laced these warnings with bloodcurdling tales about Maldek.

A controversial UFO report from Mendoza, Argentina, is rather typical of these warnings. On September 1, 1968, Carlos Peccinetti, twenty-six, and Fernando José Villegas, twenty-nine, were driving home from their job at the Mendoza casino at 3:30 A.M., when their car suddenly stalled. They got out to look under the hood and discovered a huge circular machine hovering nearby. Three beings in coveralls appeared, they said, and they found they were paralyzed, unable to move. A foreign-sounding voice rang in their heads. "It was as though they had put into our ears the tiny earplug speakers used with transistors," Peccinetti said.

"We have just made three journeys around the sun," the voice told them, "studying customs and languages of the inhabitants of the system...mathematics is the universal language."

Then a circular screen, similar to a television screen, appeared next to the object, and the two men were treated to a series of images. The first was a waterfall in lush country; the second, a mushroom-shaped cloud; the third, the waterfall scene again but without water.

After the entities clambered into the machine and flew off, the two witnesses were able to move again. Their story contains all the familiar ingredients of thousands of other UFO contact tales. First, their automobile stalled, then they were paralyzed, next they heard a telepathic voice, and finally they were given a simplified message...and the meaning of that message is quite obvious.

Police officers, doctors, lawyers, college professors, government officials, and just plain folks by the thousands have shared similar experiences in recent years. The members of WOW have really been engaged in an all-out effort to convince us of some impending disaster. It is not unusual that they should relate their warnings with tales about past civilizations that followed the same woeful path.

The Atlantis story seems to acquire another meaning in view of all this. Atlantis could be a part of our future instead of our past. Perhaps *we* are the Atlanteans.

Chapter Three

It's a Nice Place to Visit But...

SOON AFTER HE BECAME PRESIDENT of the United Arab Republic, the late Gamal Abdel Nasser ordered a giant eighty-foot statue moved from the desert to a park in Cairo. The statue had been standing for uncounted centuries near the famous Steppe Pyramid. A battery of engineers and workmen descended on it, equipped with bulldozers, tractors, and monstrous cranes. They struggled with the project for weeks, first perplexed, then annoyed, and finally humiliated by the discovery that modern technology simply could not budge the mammoth piece of stone. This raised the even more troublesome question: how had the ancient Egyptians moved the statue into place to begin with?

Archaelogists have been arguing for years about the methods employed by the ancient stonemasons. Some quite moronic theories have not only been suggested but have been widely accepted as the answer. These theories are, as usual, taught to schoolchildren. The mystery is regarded as solved. Nobody asks questions.

There are over ninety pyramids in Egypt alone. (There are dozens of others all over the world; the largest of all is located deep in China.) Most of the Egyptian pyramids were once used as the burial places for pharaohs, but the Great Pyramid at Giza was never employed for this purpose, and no one has an inkling *why* it was built. Some of the gigantic stones in these structures and in the great temples spotted around Egypt were apparently taken from quarries hundreds of miles away. The popular archaeological theory is that these stones were floated up the Nile on rafts and then moved into place on wooden rollers. Since some of these blocks weigh as much as five tons, this means that in order to float them, the Egyptians would have had to build huge rafts capable of displacing over five tons of water. Otherwise, they would just sink to the bottom with their load. The Egyptians didn't amount to much when it came to building ships. No evidence of these super-rafts has ever turned up.

There are other flaws in these theories. We are told that hundreds of thousands of slaves were pressed into pyramid building during certain seasons of each year. This leads us to the problem of logistics. It would take a complex organization to feed these hundreds of thousands daily and administer to their needs. Various modern engineers and experts have applied their slide rules to the problem, and the most liberal estimate of the time required to construct the Great Pyramid is six hundred years.

Strangely, although the ancient Egyptians left profusive records of everything else, no one has ever turned up even a single piece of papyrus describing the planning or building of these massive monuments. The stones were cut and dressed with such perfection that a piece of paper cannot be inserted between them. Obviously those early stonemasons were superb craftsmen, and obviously there were a lot of them in order to undertake and complete such enormous tasks.

When there is a mystery that can't be logically explained by science, cults develop that create explanations of their own. Our Atlantophiles naturally agree that the Egyptians didn't build the pyramids at all. Our UFO buffs claim they were built by the wonderful space people.

Morris K. Jessup, an astrophysicist and an early student of ufology, reviewed the question and suggested:

> Levitation is the only feasible answer. I believe that this lifting machine was a spaceship, probably of vast proportions; that it brought colonists to various parts of the Earth, probably from other terrestrial areas; that it supplied the heavy lift power for erecting great stone works; and that it was suddenly destroyed or taken away. Such a hypothesis would underwrite all of the movements of stone over which archaeologists and engineers have pondered.

This presents us with a splendid contradiction. If some super-society in the sky had the technology to build a spaceship "of vast proportions" and fly it all the way to our humble planet, why would they have the need to play around with stone blocks? If they wanted to leave behind evidence of their visit, they did a poor job of it, for we never have figured out the real meaning of these monoliths. Couldn't they have engraved a nice little message for us inside the Great Pyramid, explaining the whole thing in seventy-five languages? The only carvings found inside the Great Pyramid are a few little scratchings in the roof of the upper chamber that archaelogists regard as stonemason marks. Similar marks have been found in other structures. Maybe they are just the ancient equivalent of "Kilroy was here."

For centuries the spirit mediums and the percipients who have chatted with ghostly Atlanteans have told us that the Great Pyramid really contains a hidden chamber crammed with goodies that will explain everything to us when the proper time comes. Not wishing to be left out, many flying saucer contactees have repeated the same promise. An anthropologist named George Hunt Williamson wrote in the early 1950s:

> The builders of the Great Pyramid buried one of their great spaceships near the structure. It will be revealed—no doubt within a comparatively short time—that there are many secret chambers within the Great Pyramid and that its true entrance lies under the silent object that is like a lion and yet like a man...the Sphinx! It will not remain silent much longer....

On February 9, 1960, a fertilizer salesman named Reinhold Schmidt was picked up by a flying saucer and flown to Egypt, according to his pamphlet, *Edge of Tomorrow*. The friendly space people conducted him on a tour of those hidden chambers where he saw, among other things, the true cross on which Christ had died. He was also shown "thirty-two tables of a heavy-quality paper, rather dark in color...imagine my surprise when I found the events of the past, present, and future there described in modern day English, in black ink, and written in beautiful longhand."

These records indicated, Schmidt claimed, "The end of this present Earth cycle will be 1998."

So after the endless discussions of the hidden chambers in the pyramid, we finally had a genuine eyewitness who had been there and seen them.

Unless, of course, Schmidt's adventure was just another variation of the classical visits to the underground fairy palaces of yesteryear.

Science took over. In 1969 a group of American scientists headed by Dr. Luis W. Alvarez traveled to Egypt and set up expensive cosmic ray detectors around the Great Pyramid. Their theory was that any cosmic rays penetrating the pyramid and passing through hidden chambers would be recorded as moving slightly faster than ray particles traveling through solid stone. They fiddled with their gadgets for months and did get some very eccentric readings at first. But finally, in the February 6, 1970, issue of *Science,* Dr. Alvarez glumly announced that no hidden chambers had been detected with his sophisticated apparatus. The cultists all nudged each other and winked knowingly. Obviously it was all a cover-up...part of the great conspiracy to keep the truth from the public.

Men have been scratching their heads over the Great Pyramid for at least four thousand years. It has never really been dated, and it could be considerably older. Whoever built it was so clever that countless efforts to find an entrance met with failure for thousands of years. Finally, in A.D. 820, the Caliph Al Mamoun launched a full-scale attack on the structure, expecting to find it filled with treasure. His men chipped away at it, heating the stones with fires and then cooling them suddenly by pouring vinegar over them. Slowly the stones cracked and they worked their way into the pyramid until they came upon a passageway. It was completely empty.

They found a larger passageway, now known as the great gallery, which leads upwards to two small chambers. The lower chamber's entrance is so small a man must enter on his hands and knees. The upper chamber contains nothing but a crude stone tub that really doesn't resemble the elaborately designed sarcophagi used by the ancient Egyptians to entomb deceased royalty. The total absence of artifacts and hieroglyphics has given archaeologists plenty to speculate over. Some have suggested that the pyramid was used as a kind of grain elevator and that wheat was measured out in that tub. Others have tried to find astronomical significance to it.

In the mid-nineteenth century the pseudoscience of pyramidology was born. A writer named John Taylor published a book in which he concluded that the whole purpose of the structure was to preserve ancient Egyptian measurements. He was followed by an astronomer, Charles Piazzi Smyth, who extended this notion to include prophecies of the past and future. He measured every inch of the pyramid, inside and out, and every angle. In 1864 Smyth published a six-hundred-page book expounding his theories, and it caused an uproar in archaeological circles for years afterwards. A small but devoted cult still exists, still trying to validate his now thoroughly discredited concepts. Most of the literature on lost Atlantis also discusses Smyth and pyramidology. The UFO cults also have their pyramidologists. Just as the pyramids are a cornerstone in human history, they also serve as key evidence to many cults with widely diversified causes.

Aside from the few major population centers, ancient Egypt was a mud hut culture. Then as now the masses lived undernourished lives in grinding poverty. Technical skills were rare. Yet somehow they managed to quarry those gigantic stones, transport them, and put them into place with geometric precision. We *know* that the Egyptians did build the ninety odd pyramids (the village of Meroe on the Upper Nile contains dozens of pyramids alone), plus numerous great temples and tombs that are still standing. But why did they build the Great Pyramid?

The Plain of Jars in Laos has been frequently mentioned in the war dispatches from Indochina. Did you ever wonder how it got its name? The answer is obvious: it is strewn with jars...huge stone jars. Some of them are over six feet high. Some are so large they can hold six men. There are more than a thousand of these peculiar artifacts scattered around a high plateau surrounded by mountains. They were apparently carved out of limestone and granite boulders, and they've been there forever. No one seems to know who carved them, when, or why. Why would anyone bother to spend weeks carving a giant stone jar in such a remote place?

Mysterious stonemasons have left the labors all over our haunted planet. Many of these fruits make no sense at all. In Costa Rica giant stone balls have been found deep in the jungles. Some of these are as big as eight feet in diameter and weigh more than sixteen tons. They are amazingly round and smooth. Scores of smaller ones, some only a few inches in diameter, have also been found. Scientists have been unable to come up with an explanation for their purpose, although they are obviously man-made. Similar stones have been found in Mexico and Guatemala.

"One thing the scientists agree on is that the spheres must have been very important to the communities of people that made them," *Science Digest* observed in June 1967. "Using the tools they had, it must have taken many years to make just one ball, even with many men on it."

Like the jars of Laos, these balls are made of granite and limestone.

The United States is covered with strange artifacts and stone ruins of unknown origin. Every state boasts of several mysterious sites. In West Virginia are the remains of huge circular stone structures apparently predating the Indians. In many states there are ruins that archaeologists have muttered about being of Roman origin. Some of these sites have become minor local tourist attractions. Others are marked only by brief highway signs. A random few, such as Mystery Hill in North Salem, New Hampshire, have attained some celebrity.

Mystery Hill features several chambers—or tombs—topped by a gigantic Sacrificial Table weighing over four tons. It is supported on stone legs and is carefully grooved. In 1969 the New England Antiquities Research Association conducted carbon 14 tests[*] around the site and concluded that it was probably built around 1000 B.C. Recent investigations have demonstrated that some of the huge stones on Mystery Hill are carefully aligned with certain stars. Each year the sun sets directly over the Winter Solstice Monolith on the first day of winter, December 21, when viewed from the center of the site, the Sacrificial Table.

---

[*]Organic material contains radioactivity which deteriorates at a known rate. The carbon 14 test is a universally accepted method for measuring such deterioration and determining the age of the material. The test does not work on inorganic substances such as stone, of course.

The Delaware Indians have a tradition that a race of giants once inhabited the region east of the Mississippi, living in enormous cities and fortifications. There are innumerable references to giants in other Indian lore and in ancient literature all over the world, including, of course, the famous "There were giants in the earth in those days" biblical statement (Genesis 6:4). South American Indians also have many legends about giants and their special civilization. Most of the tales, no matter what the source, assert that the giants were unfriendly and even hostile to normal men. Bones of giants (who must have been eight to twelve feet tall) have been found in the mounds of Minnesota and several other places. So it is entirely possible that a race of giants did exist in earlier times, and some of these huge stone constructions may have been their handiwork. Unfortunately, science doesn't believe in giants, so all this evidence has been ignored.*

There is also considerable evidence that Christopher Columbus was a rather late arrival to the New World. He was probably preceded by the Vikings and maybe even the ancient Phoenicians. Chinese artifacts have been found in Mexico and California, so perhaps even the Chinese beat Chris by several centuries.

A knight from the Orkney Islands left a carving in Massachusetts in the fourteenth century. Near Heavener, Oklahoma, there is a stone twelve feet high, ten feet wide, and sixteen inches thick, covered with ancient Scandinavian runic symbols. It was discovered by Choctaw Indians in 1830, and archaeologists have been arguing about it ever since. Several other runestones have been found, the most famous being the Kensington Stone, found by a farmer near Kensington, Minnesota, at the turn of the century.

Two more runestones have been found in Oklahoma in recent years. The last one was discovered by two schoolboys near Poteau, Oklahoma, in September of 1967. As usual, the archaeologists are sharply divided over the validity of these discoveries. One group cries hoax, even though it would require an expert archaeologist and linguist to perpetrate such a hoax. Others,

---

*For a more detailed discussion of giants see Chapter Six, *Strange Creatures from Time and Space*.

such as Frederick Pohl, a noted Norse scholar, seem to think these stones may be authentic.*

Fifty years before Columbus conned Queen Isabella into financing his expedition, someone drew up a rough map of North America. A copy of this map was discovered by Laurence Whitten, a rare book dealer from New Haven, Connecticut, in 1957. It is now part of the rare document collection in the Beinecke Library of Yale University and is known as the Yale Vinland Map. Scientific investigators have dated it at A.D. 1440, and as usual, the leading experts have been arguing about it ever since. Some have branded it an out-and-out hoax, while others regard it as further evidence that the Vikings were frequent visitors to the New World.

More substantial evidence has been found in the form of ruins of a Viking longhouse on the Ungava Peninsula in northern Canada. A team from Laval University has dated it between the eleventh and twelfth centuries. Numerous other ruins and artifacts have been found all over North America. For example, two remarkably similar axes, both apparently of medieval European origin, have been discovered in Beardmore, Ontario, and Rocky Nook Point, Massachusetts.

Archaeologists from the Smithsonian Institution uncovered a small slab of stone covered with ciphers in 1885 near Bat Creek, Tennessee. They decided it was probably the work of Cherokee Indians, but modern specialists such as Dr. Joseph B. Mahan of the Museum of Arts and Crafts at Columbus, Georgia, have taken a second look at it and disputed the old Indian theory. Dr. Mahan knows Cherokee and he persuaded the Smithsonian to re-examine the Bat Creek stone. "You simply can't ignore evidence," Dr. Mahan stated, "just because it doesn't fit current theory."

A similar stone was found by Manfred Metcalf at Fort Benning, Georgia, in 1968. Metcalf was looking for stones to build a barbecue grill in his backyard when he unearthed the stone. It is nine inches square and covered with triangles, circles, and straight and wavy lines. He passed it on to Dr. Mahan, who thought the markings appeared to be characteristically

---

*See Frederick Pohl, *The Viking Explorers*.

Mediterranean. Another scientist, Dr. Cyrus H. Gordon, chairman of Mediterranean studies at Brandeis University, agreed. There were strong similarities between the Metcalf stone and samples of Minoan writing dating back three thousand years to the Bronze Age civilization that flourished on the Mediterranean island of Crete from 3000 to 1100 B.C. Dr. Gordon became the center of another controversy a few years ago when he announced that a sample of Phoenician writing found on a stone in Brazil was authentic...after other archaeologists had denounced it as a fraud. After all, it was hardly possible that the ancient Phoenicians could have visited Brazil. Or was it?

As for the Bat Creek stone, Dr. Gordon thinks it might have been the handiwork of Hebrews from Palestine during the Bronze Age. Both scientists speculate that ancient Semitic tribes from the Middle East may have visited North America thousands of years ago. This, of course, revives memories of the lost tribes of Israel. Could they have somehow found their way to this continent and become that lost American culture described in the Mormon Bible? Dr. Mahan believes that some Indian tribes can be traced back to seafaring Mediterranean peoples. The Yuchi, he points out, are racially and linguistically different from other North American tribes. Their legends state, "We came as the sun came, and we went as the sun went." Dr. Mahan interprets this to mean that the Yuchi came from the east, across the Atlantic Ocean, and then moved northwards from Florida to Georgia.

Some archaeologists tend to lump runestones together with the stones bearing Indian petroglyphs. Petroglyphs are designs carved into rocks as pathmarkers, and thousands have been found all over the Americas. Although innumerable isolated Indian tribes were obviously responsible for them, there are many interesting similarities in the symbols used. Some of these same symbols have been found carved on other ancient rocks in other parts of the world, suggesting that this form of writing was universal at one time...even though the races and tribes responsible could not understand each other's languages and in most cases had little or no contact. Archaeologists studiously try to overlook the fact that some of these pictographs can be traced to ancient Mediterranean cultures. But the runic writing is quite distinct from the Indian petroglyphs. The runestones carry alphabetic symbols, while pet-roglyphs bear picture writing loosely related to the Egyptian hieroglyphs.

The Kensington stone, as translated by Frederick Pohl, describes how "eight Goths and twenty-two Norwegians" established a camp. One group went fishing, and when they returned, they found the ten who had remained behind "red with blood and dead." The year is given as 1362. Indian petro-glyphs, on the other hand, were customarily devoted to trail information, where to find water, and the like.

One Indian pictograph of particular interest is a complex design that has been found throughout North, Central, and South America. It depicts a series of squares inside one another. The Hopi Indians call this the Mother Earth Symbol. To the Pimas it is the House of Teuhu; to the Cunas in Panama it is the Tree of Life. Anthropologist Harold Sterling Gladwin saw something else in it when he studied this symbol carved on the wall of Casa Grande, Arizona. In his book, *Men Out of Asia*, he noted that the Mother Earth symbol is iden-tical with the Minoan labyrinth depicted on coins from Knossos, Crete, circa 200 B.C. The famous labyrinth was said to have been built by Daedalus to hide the half-man, half-bull Minotaur. Dr. Gladwin and Dr. Clyde Keeler of Milledgeville, Georgia, both seem to think that the Indians' use of the ancient labyrinth symbol is evidence of the influence of the early Minoan culture.

In the early 1960s Angelos Galanopoulos, a Greek scientist, proposed still another theory for Atlantis. He suggested that sunken Minoan cities of Crete might have supplied the basis for the Atlantis legends. According to his theory, Plato got his dates wrong. Atlantis may have disappeared only a thousand or so years before the historian heard the tale, not nine thousand years before. It may have been one of the Greek islands, possi-bly Thera.

Divers and archaeologists working in the waters there in recent years have uncovered all kinds of evidence indicating that the Minoan culture came to a very abrupt end. So abrupt that craftsmen left their tools next to unfin-ished works and fled. The explanation currently in vogue is that a sudden volcanic eruption destroyed the islands. Dr. Galanopoulos has been partially successful in matching Plato's description of Atlantis with what is now known about Thera. Dr. Bruce C. Heezen, an oceanographer, believes that the eruption occurred around 1400 B.C. Needless to say, other scientists and scholars loudly dispute this date.

We do know that early Crete was the center of an impressive culture, that great cities and temples were built there, and that it was a major naval power. It is not likely, however, that Crete and Thera could have lived up to Plato's description of the supercivilization of Atlantis.

Still we have all the perplexing evidence of the runestones and other artifacts scattered around this continent, which demonstrate that men from Europe and possibly from Crete and Thera did visit America in pre-Columbian times. It is even possible that groups settled here and built forts and temples, the remnants of which have served to augment the beliefs of dozens of cults and fringe societies.

In a learned dissertation on petroglyphs published by the Smithsonian in 1937, Julian H. Steward frowned on the arguments that attempt to prove that "Egyptians, Scythians, Chinese, and a host of other Old World peoples, including the Ten Lost Tribes of Israel, invaded America in ancient days." He noted that "devotees of the subject have written voluminously, argued bitterly, and even fought duels."

Now, over thirty years later, the Smithsonian is slowly changing its tune. They have stopped blaming the Indians for all these carved slabs. The Indians have been denying credit all along, of course.

"When the white men first arrived here [in British Columbia, Canada] in 1860, the West Coast Indians had already incorporated the carvings in their legends," Phil Thornburg, a petroglyph expert in Victoria, Canada, said recently. "They showed them to white explorers and explained they were left by an ancient civilization and were the hub of creation."

Thornburg points to what appears to be a carving of a Chinese dragon, known in Indian legend as a *sisutl*. "There does seem to be an Oriental background to them," he observes. "Being carved in sandstone, it's virtually impossible to say what age they are. I've found some that were buried under more than a foot of topsoil.

"Now this wasn't the kind of topsoil that would have washed over them. This was formed there, placing the age of the carving around five to seven thousand years—which is really ancient for this country."

Thornburg found one petroglyph on Vancouver Island that had a hole worn completely through it by dripping water—proof that it had been there for a very long time. At another site he found a carving that had crumbled when a massive tree grew straight up through it.

Petroglyphs that were definitely the work of Indian tribes often tell interesting stories about hunts and battles, and in several instances encounters with the little people and other phantom inhabitants. Some contain solemn warnings that the valley or mountain ahead is the abode of these sinister phantoms.

The Cherokee Indians have legends about the strange entities who resided around Chimney Rock, North Carolina. White people have also seen them occasionally. In 1806 the Rev. George Newton reported to the *Raleigh Register* "a very extraordinary vision of thousands of beings in the air. They possessed a glittering appearance resembling the human form and were seen on or about Chimney Rock on the thirty-first of July last." Researcher Angelo Capparello found this testimony by a Mrs. Reaves, one of the alleged witnesses:

> I looked towards the Chimney. I was absolutely amazed, for south of Chimney Rock and floating along the side of the mountain was a huge crowd of white, phantomlike beings. Their clothing (and filmy as it looked, I can only call it "clothing") was so brilliant a white it almost hurt my eyes to look at them...Although I felt weak, somehow, it left a solemn and pleasing impression on my mind.

Chimney Rock is only one of the countless haunted places on this haunted planet.

Chapter Four

Towers of Glass and Theories of Putty

VITRIFY IS A TEN-DOLLAR WORD meaning to change into glass. Glass is made by heating sand (silica) and/or various oxides of silicon, boron, phosphorus, and other materials, then cooling the result rapidly to prevent crystallization. The process is fairly simple, and men have been manufacturing glass for thousands of years. When the first atomic bomb was exploded in New Mexico in 1945, it not only left a big hole in the ground, but the tremendous heat melted the sand and fused it together in glasslike fragments. These scorched particles were identical to the objects known as tektites. Tektites have been found all over our haunted planet and have baffled science for years. One recent expedition found tektites scattered over an area six thousand by four thousand miles from Tasmania to north of the Philippines and from the East Indies to the east coast of Africa. These were analyzed as being approximately seven hundred thousand years old.* To see what a tektite looks like, go to the Museum of Natural History in New York.

Like nature, science abhors a vacuum. So most books on mineralogy blandly assert that tektites are of "meteoric origin." It is a nice little theory, and everybody seems to believe it. However, a majority of all meteorites are made out of solid iron, and most are vaporized by the intense heat of friction when they enter our atmosphere. Substances capable of melting into glass would, of course, burn up before they hit the surface of the earth.

---

*See "Tektites and Geomagnetic Reversals," B. P. Glass and Bruce C. Heezen, *Scientific American:* July, 1967.

In 1969 a group of NASA scientists dished up a delicious new version of the meteorite theory. They announced that tektites were from the moon. Aeons ago, they speculated, a huge meteor plummeted into the moon, striking with such force that its impact hurled tons of moon dust into space. This lunar material attained escape velocity and passed into an orbit around the earth, where it gradually was sucked downwards by gravity, entered the earth's atmosphere, melted, and fell into the Pacific Ocean. So another mystery was solved...unless you happen to have an eighth-grade education, a slide rule, and a basic knowledge of the mechanics involved. Then you would find that the impacting meteor would have to be of enormous size and be traveling at fantastic velocity in order to accomplish the first step—casting debris beyond the moon's gravity. Such a meteor would, in all probability, affect the moon in other discernible ways—such as changing its orbit. Next, a long series of spectacular coincidences would be necessary for the debris to enter the proper orbit at the proper time so that it would lapse into a retrograde orbit around the earth. Finally, since tons of tektites are scattered in paths across the Pacific floor, and since we know that less than five percent of a mass entering the earth's atmosphere is likely to survive and hit the surface, the quantity of lunar material necessary to produce those tektites must have been larger than the original impacting meteor.

Hunks of glass have fallen from the sky, however. In fact, since ancient times all kinds of odd junk has been dropping on us, ranging from stone pillars and metal wheels to huge blocks of ice and vast quantities of real blood and even raw meat. Science conveniently ignores everything but the iron lumps which, they presume, are pieces of old planets drifting around in space. To astronomy's credit, we do know that there are groups of this debris in the earth's orbit around the sun, and we can predict annual meteor showers that occur as we pass through this mess.

One chunk of glass and metal crashed into a driveway in Cannifton, Ontario, in September of 1968. Wesley Reid looked at it and saw that it was too hot to handle. After it cooled, he found he had a brownish object weighing about twelve ounces. When it was tested by experts, they found it was made of glass laced with a small quantity of pure zinc. Whatever it was, it didn't seem to be a part of a man-made satellite (which would contain very little glass anyway), and it definitely fell out of the sky.

Earth's phantom inhabitants are always dumping their garbage on us. Flying saucer enthusiasts have been collecting and analyzing this junk for years and have found pieces of pure aluminum, magnesium, tin, copper, slag, and endless varieties of silicon. Unfortunately for them, none of this aerial debris seems to support their contention that UFOs are spaceships from another planet. Nor has any known meteorite strewn such materials or tektites in its path.

The discovery of tektites and vitrified stones among the ancient ruins of Baalbek has inspired another popular ufological myth: that Baalbek once served as a spaceport for rocket ships from another world. A Soviet ethnologist, Professor M. Agrest, proposed the theory in an article in Moscow's *Literaturnaya Gazeta* in 1959. He also suggested that Sodom and Gomorrah were destroyed by an atomic bomb. Lot's wife, he asserted, did not turn into a pillar of salt but was actually reduced to a pile of ashes when she ignored a warning not to linger behind Lot's fleeing party.

Baalbek is located in Lebanon, east of Beirut and north of Damascus, Syria. In ancient times it was a thriving city filled with great temples dedicated to Baal, the sun god. The pillars and stone slabs (some weighing many tons) still standing are impressive...but no more impressive than the scores of other similar ruins scattered throughout the Middle East. Enormous ruins of this type can be found deep in the heart of inhospitable deserts, raising once again the question of how the ancient peoples managed to quarry, transport, and erect these monuments with crude tools and a minimum of mechanical aids. Yet, quite obviously, they did manage...and managed well.

In 1948 an expedition from the University of Chicago unearthed the remnants of an ancient village thirty miles east of Kirkuk, Iraq. Dr. Robert J. Braidwood estimated that the village had been settled some eight thousand years ago. Baalbek is, in comparison, a modern city.

Professor Agrest's theories were a bombshell to the assorted cults, particularly the flying saucer believers. He regarded the presence of tektites as evidence that atomic powered rockets had once used the vast stone platforms at Baalbek as launching areas. Apparently he did not know that vitrified ruins are a common phenomenon all over the world. Forts and towers so old that there are no legends to account for them can be found throughout northern Europe and the British Isles and the walls of many of these are vitrified. At some point in the distant past these structures must have been subjected to tremendous heat, though not necessarily from the blast of some nuclear powered rocket.

Lightning is the explanation most frequently offered by science. But there is no evidence to indicate that lightning bolts vitrify stone or even sand, although we really know very little about lightning and its effects. It would take dozens of lightning bolts all striking the same spot to produce these vitrified monuments. In some parts of the world, such as an area of eighteen thousand square yards outside of Cuzco, Peru, whole hillsides have been vitrified. Theories of volcanic activity and glacial movements have been offered to account for these, but none of these theories really work.

There are legends describing how the planet was once bathed in fire. Maybe more than once. So this vitrification could be the product of some nearly forgotten natural catastrophe.

On October 8, 1871, a gigantic fireball or meteor roared over the Midwest, causing a rash of disastrous fires in several states, including the famous Chicago fire. Thousands of people were killed in Illinois and Wisconsin, and vast areas were ravaged by flames that night. A similar fiery visitor from space could have caused the vitrifications.*

Another strange phenomenon could be to blame. From time to time overpowering waves of heat from an unknown source are concentrated in specific areas. Figueira, Portugal, suffered one of these mysterious blasts of heat for two minutes on July 6, 1949. The temperature soared to 158 degrees. Hundreds of people collapsed in the streets, while thousands of chickens and ducks keeled over dead, and the Mondego River dried up suddenly in several places, killing countless fish. We don't understand this phenomenon at

---

*See *Mysterious Fires and Lights* by Vincent Gaddis for a fully documented description of the 1871 catastrophe.

all, and it is possible that even more intense heat waves of this type have occurred in the past.

The followers of Agrest were not about to accept such mundane explanations for the vitrification of Baalbek, however. A young astronomer, Dr. Carl Sagan, presented a paper before the American Rocket Society on November 15, 1962, in which he repeated Professor Agrest's speculations and urged that ancient myths and legends be re-examined for possible clues to an early visit by an extraterrestrial civilization. Other researchers scoured the ancient records of India and found things such as the Mahabharata, a document dating back more than three thousand years, which describes a "blazing missile" that hurtled out of the sky into the midst of an attacking army, producing "a radiance of smokeless fire" that flattened chariots, ignited forests, boiled rivers, and produced dark clouds of death. All of this sounded uneasily like an atomic attack. In the *Mausala Parva* another ancient historical account, there is a vivid description of some kind of death-dealing ray that began as a small, bright glow, grew into a shaft of brilliant light, and then consumed its target. This phenomenon was accompanied by violent winds, peals of thunder in cloudless skies, and earth tremors. Terrible *rakshashas*, shaped like huge mounds, attacked another Indian army from the sky and fired "weapons winged with gold," thunderbolts, and hundreds of fiery wheels.

Even in the Bible we are told how the prophet Elijah was saved by balls of fire that wiped out a hundred soldiers and their captains (II Kings 1). That would have been around 896 B.C. There are innumerable stories of this type from all cultures, indicating that WOW is armed with spectacularly advanced weapons and doesn't hesitate to use them against mortal men. So one cultist conclusion about the vitrified forts is that they were attacked by flying saucers that focused deadly heat rays on them and their occupants. However, the entire desert between Damascus and Baghdad is littered with blackened rocks. Thousands of square miles seem to be charred, not by the sun but by some long forgotten holocaust. Did WOW lay waste to all of Mesopotamia? Or did some horrible natural disaster wipe out the great civilization that once thrived there?

Chapter Five

Strong Men and
Stupid Enterprises

FOUR THOUSAND YEARS AGO Great Britain was populated by a small group of people barely out of the Stone Age. They had a few primitive tools made of bones, and they probably eked out a living with only the greatest difficulty. Anthropologists estimate that there were probably about three hundred thousand of them. They were undoubtedly divided into warring clans and factions, since factionalism is a natural state of man. Yet somehow, thousands of these people managed to get together to spend many generations quarrying huge stones (some weighing thirty tons) in the Prescelly Mountains of Wales and hauling these enormous blocks 240 miles to Amesbury. There they systematically arranged these stones in a circle, following measurements so precise that they were able to construct a mathematically correct astronomical computer.

It's called Stonehenge.

Like the Great Pyramid, Stonehenge appears to have been a pointless and impossible exercise. Thousands of workers had to be fed, clothed, and housed for generations as they labored on the profitless project. Top-flight administrative talent must have been necessary to plan and organize the work and supervise its execution. Architects had to design the monument with care before the first block of stone was chipped out of the hillside. Above all, we are asked (by the archaeologists) to believe that these early primitives had the motivation necessary to dedicate themselves to such an awesome task. We are also asked to believe that they pushed and hauled these monstrous stones up and down hills, across rivers, through forests and soupy bogs on sledges and wooden rollers. Then, somehow, they managed to stand the slabs on end, lifted other stones on top of them, and built the whole thing so securely that it would last for four thousand years.

Plainly, the whole thing is quite absurd.

In his definitive book, *Stonehenge Decoded*, astronomer Gerald S. Hawkins catalogs these absurdities and offers the educated estimate that the construction of Stonehenge required at least 1.5 million man-days of physical labor. He calculates that it took three centuries to build. That's ten generations. Ten generations of primitive people who were somehow convinced that it was worthwhile to arrange a pile of giant stones in a circle on an English plain.

"For generations the work on Salisbury plain must have absorbed most of the energies—physical, mental, spiritual—and most of the material resources of a whole people," Hawkins observes.

There are others, of course, who prefer to believe that the early Britons didn't build Stonehenge at all. To them, it is obviously the work of the Atlanteans or even the wondrous space people.

If Stonehenge were the only existing megalithic monument of this type in Britain, Hawkins' work would be more acceptable. Unfortunately, there are *several hundred* of these stone circles scattered about the British Isles, many of them just as mysterious as Stonehenge. We must therefore assume that all the Stone Age Britons were frantically engaged in monument building for at least a thousand years. If the scientists have dated Stonehenge correctly, then its construction occurred around the same time that the Minoan culture blossomed on distant Crete. The Great Pyramid had already been built or was in the final stages. So far as we can tell, the Indians had not yet appeared in North and South America.

On Lewis, the northernmost island of the Outer Hebrides, many hundreds of miles north of Stonehenge, there is another group of giant standing stones arranged in a circle. Called Callanish, this ring consists of thirteen blocks set around a large central stone. It is erected in a desolate, hard-to-reach place, again posing the questions, how and why did the early builders put it there? Since Callanish is somewhat cruder than Stonehenge, Hawkins speculates that perhaps it was built first, and the builders applied what they had learned from that effort to the later construction on the Salisbury Plain. But the two sites are separated by a vast distance and expanses of water. In order for the theory to work, we need evidence that the early Britons were also great travelers and had a society developed enough so that they could travel in large groups. The small, wandering tribes couldn't meet these criteria.

Astronomers and scientists have been measuring and studying these sites for centuries, and the general conclusion is that the stones were arranged in such a way that they deliberately aligned with certain stars and phases of the moon to form a crude computer that acted as a calendar. Hawkins fed his own calculations into a modern electronic computer and produced numerous charts and tables demonstrating such correlations. In essence, when a man stands in the center of the Stonehenge circle, specific stars (or the sun or moon) appear directly over specific stones at specific times of the year in a manner that had to be planned by the builders. Hawkins concluded:

> Some 240 Stonehenge alignments translated into celestial declinations. For whatever reasons those Stonehenge builders built as they did, their final, completed creation was a marvel. As intricately aligned as an interlocking series of astronomical observing instruments (which indeed it was) and yet architecturally perfectly simple, in function subtle and elaborate, in appearance stark, imposing, awesome, Stonehenge was a thing of surpassing ingenuity of design, variety of usefulness, and grandeur—in concept and construction an eighth wonder of the ancient world.

Considering the enormous amount of effort that must have gone into its construction, Stonehenge ranks as the costliest calendar in the world.

Earlier investigators tried to explain Stonehenge as the work of the Romans, the Danes (similar constructions stand in Denmark), and the Druids, as esoteric priesthood that entered Britain from France in 500 B.C. Stonehenge had been around for at least one thousand years when the Druids arrived, but nevertheless, Druidism has become closely allied with Stonehenge. Even today, members of the Most Ancient Order of Druids make an annual pilgrimage to the site to perform their rites—rites that they claim date back to the days of Atlantis, incidentally.

Hawkins discovered that a significant cycle occurs every 113.6 years at Stonehenge. He calls it midwinter moonrise, for the moon rises over one particular stone every 18.6 years. Then he points out with some glee a statement by the ancient historian Diodorus (circa 50 B.C.): "The Moon as viewed from this island appears to be but a little distance from the earth and to have on it prominences like those of the earth, which are visible to the eye. The account is also given that the god visits the island every nineteen years, the period in which the return of the stars to the same place in the heavens is accomplished."

What god visited the British Isles every nineteen years? Could Stonehenge have been constructed to predict the appearances of some alien being? This would have given those ancient stonemasons a strong religious motive for constructing it.

Whoever planned Stonehenge had to have a knowledge of mathematics and astronomy. Did the Stone Age Britons possess such knowledge? Or was the information passed along to them somehow? Were they following orders, just as Moses followed the specifications given to him by Jehovah for the construction of a gold ark (Exodus 25)? The gods and demons of all cultures have always had a penchant for ordering men to build huge, seemingly useless temples, tombs, and artifacts.

Soon after Gerald Hawkins published a summary of his findings in *Nature,* October 26, 1963, he became the center of controversy. Mathematicians, astronomers, and archaeologists who had never been near Stonehenge assaulted his thesis and dissected his semantics. He did leave many unanswered questions—largely because they are unanswerable.

Twenty miles from Stonehenge there is another ancient wonder…the mammoth mound at Silbury. This is a man-made mound of earth 130 feet high, covering over five acres. Scientists estimate that it was constructed around 1800 B.C., which means that while thousands of early Britons were starting work on Stonehenge, other hundreds or thousands were pointlessly hauling baskets of dirt to Silbury to build one of the largest mounds on earth. In 1848, a group of investigators burrowed a tunnel into it, going from the top to the bottom in hope of finding some clue. All they discovered were some picks made from red deer antlers. Recently these objects were given the carbon 14 test and were found to be from around 800 B.C. This was most upsetting to the theorists who believed the mound was at least a thousand years older than that. At the present time a team of American and British archaeologists are busy digging new holes in the Silbury mound, searching for new clues.

Man-made mounds of unknown origin and purpose number in the thousands all over this haunted planet. In Ireland, they are called *sidhe*, or fairy mounds, and are purportedly the homes of the little people. St. Patrick is supposed to have stood on Croagh Patrick, a mound in County Mayo, when he ordered the snakes out of Ireland. Hundreds of these mounds are scattered throughout the United States, where they are popularly called "Indian mounds," even though the Indians have no legends to account for them. Some of the mounds in Ohio, Minnesota, and in the Southwest are skillfully laid out in geometric patterns that can be seen only from the air. When viewed from above, they represent elephants, birds, snakes, and other animals. Whoever laid these things out apparently intended them to be seen from the air. From the ground they appear to be nothing more than symmetrical hills with flat tops.

Aerial surveys of South America have revealed elaborate, ridged fields and earthworks (some covering fifty thousand acres and some as long as a thousand miles) in at least five scattered locations. The ridged field at Lake Titicaca in the Andes covers two hundred thousand acres and is spread over 160 miles. These man-made ridges and mounds may have been part of a complex agricultural and irrigation system.*

Other mounds and ridges of this sort are spread throughout Europe and Asia. Stone chests found in mounds in the Mississippi Valley are identical to chests dug up in mounds in Yorkshire, England. But most of the mounds have yielded little or nothing to patient diggers. Yet the presence of these

---

*See "Pre-Columbian Ridged Fields," J. J. Parsons and W. M. Denevan, *Scientific American,* July 1967.

mounds everywhere is an indication of a worldwide culture in prehistoric times that regarded mound building as an important activity.

We do know that mound building persisted as part of the burial rites of ancient peoples. Early historians such as Homer and Herodotus describe these rites. Alexander the Great is supposed to have spent a fortune to erect a huge mound over the grave of his friend, Hephaestion. The kings of ancient Scythia on the Black Sea were buried under mounds. Archaeologists assume that this mound-building practice led eventually to the development of the Egyptian pyramids. The desert sand was a poor mound-making material, so the Egyptians switched to stone blocks. But how did mound building spread to the Americas in the pre-Indian epoch?

Flying saucer cultists read great significance into the fact that many modern UFO sightings seem to congregate around the old "Indian" mounds. Strange lights, bobbing and weaving and blinking in intelligent patterns, periodically cavort above the mounds of the Ohio and Mississippi valleys. Since UFOs have a tendency to appear in the same geographical locations year after year, century after a century, it is possible that ancient peoples saw them too, and erected the mounds for them. Some flying saucer writers have borrowed a page from Prof. Agrest's Baalbek theory and suggested that the flat-topped mounds were intended as UFO airports.

If the great mounds were merely monuments to the dead, they were costly ones. Even with modern bulldozers and steamshovels, it would take much time and money to construct a mound 130 feet high and five acres square, like the Silbury mound. It is difficult to visualize tribes of prehistoric people engaging in this activity for months or years. It is even more difficult to think of them planning the mounds so they would present specific symbols when seen from the air.

Now it has been established that while the early Britons were simultaneously erecting Stonehenge and piling dirt for the Silbury mound, they were also carving giant figures in nearby hillsides. The figure of a great white horse is cut into the summit of a hill in the Berkshire Downs. At Cerne Abbas, a giant "cave man" is traced upon a hillside. He carries a club, and his male genitalia are prominently displayed. A similar figure, the Long Man at Wilmington, was emasculated by early Christians. There are many others spotted from Australia to Africa to the United States, all obviously meant to serve as landmarks for unknown pilots cruising the virgin skies. The tradition for making these landmarks survived until at least fifteen hundred years ago, for that is the apparent age of the famous Nazca Lines found in the Peruvian desert. Nobody paid much attention to these lines until the early 1940s. Since then they have become an important facet of Atlantean and flying saucer lore.

From ground level the Nazca Lines are merely a jumble of paths made by brushing aside the stones and pebbles of the desert. There is little rain or natural erosion in the area, so the lines have remained intact far at least seven hundred years and possibly even for fifteen hundred (estimates vary). Seen from the air, the clearances form the outlines of spiders, birds, fish, assorted monsters or unknown animals, and numerous squares and rectangles, some longer than two football fields. Dr. Maria Reiche, a German astronomer, lived at Nazca for forty years beginning in the 1950s, carefully charting all the lines by viewing them atop a high ladder. Daniel Cohen remarked in *Science Digest*, May 1970:

> In spite of such devotion to her work, she is regarded by some scientists as a woman obsessed with a theory, rather than a careful scientist. Dr. Reiche has produced all sorts of correlations between the lines and the positions of the sun, moon, and stars. She postulates a gigantic "desert calendar" with which the ancient Peruvians could mark the passing of the years. Her opponents argue that with so many lines and so many astronomical bodies with which to make alignments, it is possible to work up many correlations, but that they are meaningless.

The Inca-Nazca people who created these lines were massacred in the wars that followed Francisco Pizarro's invasion of Peru in the 1500s. The Inca civilization destroyed by Pizarro apparently came along centuries after the lines were laid out. An ancient Inca road slices across, severing the lines. It would seem that the Incas regarded the lines as insignificant. Nevertheless, hundreds of people have worked for years, if not for generations, in planning these lines and scratching away at them. The Nazca Lines remain as another of early man's energetic but seemingly pointless enterprises.

On Easter Sunday, 1722, Dutch admiral Jaakob Rogeveen landed on an island in the Pacific some twenty-two hundred miles from the coast of South America. The first things he saw were hundreds of giant statues squatting near the water line, staring out to sea. They were huge, eyeless heads mounted on small stone bodies. Some were as high as thirty-six feet.

Admiral Rogeveen had discovered not Atlantis, but Easter Island...a pitifully barren volcanic island with an area of forty-five square miles, with almost no trees, and with no wildlife except for hordes of bothersome insects. It was populated by cannibalistic tribes of Polynesian origin who had apparently migrated there centuries before. The current population is 270, but at one time it was considerably larger. Intertribal wars and raids by early slave traders whittled the population down.

The *ahu* statues were quarried from volcanic rock. Some weigh as much as thirty tons. Since wood is practically nonexistent on the island, the statues must have been hauled out of the quarries with ropes and sheer muscle power, dragged down to the beaches, and raised upright with more muscle power. Many of the monuments were topped with a hat, or *pukao*, made out of red rock. Some of these *pukaos* weighed five tons. How the natives raised these five-ton carvings to the tops of the erected statues is another puzzle.

Like the builders of Stonehenge, the Easter Islanders had to accomplish their task with the crudest kind of tools. Each statue must represent months or years of labor. There are over six hundred on the island. The statue-building came to an abrupt end for some reason. So abrupt that the workers dropped their stone chisels on the spot. Their tools have been found in the quarry, next to two hundred unfinished statues, some of which measure sixty-six feet long.

Various expeditions have visited Easter Island and tried to piece together the story of the *ahu* builders, but the surviving natives have only the vaguest legends. During the tribal conflicts of the eighteenth and nineteenth centuries, many of the statues were overturned and destroyed rather contemptuously. Remnants of the island's culture were erased by the wars, slavers, a smallpox epidemic, and missionaries who ordered the destruction of pagan artifacts. The latter included ancient wooden tablets covered with an unknown form of writing. Only a few samples of these tablets remain in scattered museums.

Scientists who have concluded that the Easter Islanders are Polynesians blithely overlook the fact that megalithic structures are virtually unknown in Polynesia and that the Polynesians never developed a form of writing. One Easter Island legend stresses that wars were waged between a tribe of long-eared people and a tribe of short ears. The short ears won and presumably ate all the long ears. Perhaps the long ears were the *ahu* builders.

Easter Island is so isolated that the early settlers must have been marooned there, and lacking wood for boatbuilding, remained out of touch with the rest of the world for centuries while they developed their own peculiar culture. They did have a complicated religion, and it is possible that the statues were some part of it. The red hats could have some meaning, for even the American Indians have legends and prophecies about gods in red hats. But there are also intriguing legends of red-haired beings in such distant and isolated places as Borneo, and the ancient gods of Europe and Asia were often described as having red or blond hair. Modern UFO contactees claim that the space people who ride around in flying saucers have long red or blond hair, too. So it is not surprising that some cultists speculate that members from WOW may have visited Easter Island and that the *ahu* statues are tributes to them, each statue symbolizing one appearance of a god.

Scores of giant, red-haired mummies have been found in a cave twenty-two miles from Lovelock, Nevada, in the last eighty years. The first ones, discovered in 1912, were between 6.5 and 7 feet tall. Artifacts found in the same cave have been dated by carbon-14 tests. Apparently, the cave had been occupied as far back as five thousand years. The local Piute Indians have legends about these giants, describing them as being cannibalistic. In her book, *Life Among the Piutes* (1882), Sarah Winnemucca Hopkins wrote that the last of the red-haired giants were exterminated by the Piutes in the nineteenth century. "They would dig large holes in our trails at night," Mrs. Hopkins reported. "Our people would fall into these holes...That tribe would even eat their own dead. Yes, they would even come and dig up our dead after they were buried and would carry them off and eat them."

Atlantis lore also describes giant red-haired cannibals who behaved almost like traditional vampires. Some authors have speculated that the red-haired giants invaded Easter Island from South America, and the cannibalistic rites of the Easter Islanders were inherited from them.

Until the early 1990s, there was an American military base on Easter Island. During its construction, the workmen and heavy equipment building an airfield were diverted to raise one of the flattened statues. It took a heavy crane to do the job that was once done by hundreds of dedicated natives engaged in another of early man's impressive but pointless enterprises.

Easter Island has been a favorite of *National Geographic* for years, and the cultists have had a field day inventing explanations for the mystery. But there are many other Pacific islands even more remote and very rarely visited that pose far more baffling questions. The city of Metalanim on the southeastern shore of Ponape Island in Micronesia is now in ruins, but it once could have housed two million people. No one knows who built it or when. Some of the stone blocks in those ruins weigh fifteen tons, and the stone used in the city is not from the island. Gigantic waterways or canals intersect the city, some of them large enough to float a battleship. Who built this enormous place, and how did they move those huge stone blocks across the Pacific to the island? Whatever happened to the two million residents?

Three thousand miles to the southeast of Ponape Island, on tiny Maiden Island in the Line Island chain, there are the ruins of forty stone temples whose architecture is identical to that of Metalanim. Basalt roads lead from these ruins straight into the Pacific Ocean. The island is uninhabited and covered with guano (bird droppings). But if we draw an imaginary line southwards from Maiden for twelve hundred miles, we arrive at Rarotonga in the Cook Islands. Here another ancient road of basalt blocks rises out of the ocean.

Innumerable other hard-to-reach islands scattered throughout the Pacific are dotted with enigmatic ruins, canals, and roadways from some long lost culture. They all seem to be interrelated, as if they were all once part of some great civilization. It would be prohibitively expensive to organize a proper scientific expedition to visit and study all of these far-flung ruins systematically. Besides, their existence doesn't fit in with any of the current anthropological theories. Suppose some scientist should find that they date back ten thousand years or more and are the remnants of some supercivilization of the past? No matter how substantial his evidence might be, he would be immediately crucified by his colleagues and drummed out of all the scientific societies.

Obviously, Metalanim was built by cannibals with stone chisels, and those canals served their religious rites to the water gods.

Believers in the lost continents of Mu, Pan, and Lemuria (which may have been one place) noisily embrace these tidbits as evidence that a great land mass did exist in the Pacific at one time and that it was populated by a highly advanced race while the Egyptians, Britons, and Cretans were all fashioning stone axes. One cultist tradition, passed along by talkative elementals and members of WOW, is that Lemuria preceded Atlantis. After Lemuria sank into the Pacific, the Atlantis culture got underway and flourished for 14,000 years before it, too, sank 10,500 years ago.*

A mystical archaeologist named James Churchward was largely responsible for the modern revival of interest in Mu. In the early part of this century, he traveled through Central and South America probing into ancient ruins and trying to decipher stone carvings and petroglyphs. Then he published a series of books that combined scientism and sciolism (that is, he applied the scientific method to dubious fragments of evidence) to support his contention that a supercontinent once existed in the Pacific. In his view, Easter Island served as a kind of factory, and the great stone heads manufactured there were shipped off to other parts of Mu. The poorly investigated ruins of the Pacific islands and the great island mounds (yes, huge man-made mounds are found on many of these islands) were all a part of that ancient civilization, he said. He leaned on scrambled translations of stone carvings and vague legends of undefined origin. These were mixed in with the flat statements of elementals and strange "wise men."

---

*See Eklal Kueshana, *The Ultimate Frontier.*

Churchward also saw evidence or traces of Mu in the Mayan civilization of Central America and the Aztec and Incan cultures further south. He
compiled charts that compared the writing of Maya with the hieroglyphs of
Egypt, and he constructed the ancient alphabet of Mu. Ultimately, he produced precise maps of Mu and tried to demonstrate how the mysterious ruins
found in the United States were linked to that remote continent. Sciolists
everywhere leaped onto his bandwagon, and an enormous body of Mu literature has developed, but science remains unconvinced.

Actually, there is considerable merit in Churchward's evidence, even
though his conclusions and his bold statements about Mu history can be
questioned. A fantastic culture of stone builders and mound builders, predating modern man by centuries or even thousands of years, obviously did
exist all over this planet. The only possible explanation for the many Pacific
ruins, such as the huge stone arch found on the coral atoll of Tonga-Tabu
(two upright columns weighing seventy tons each, topped by a crosspiece
weighing twenty-five tons), is that these islands must have somehow been
linked together by a land mass in the distant past. The culture of this mysterious land spread throughout the world. Then an unthinkable catastrophe
occurred. A catastrophe that altered the face of the whole earth and wiped
out everything but the most durable constructions of that doomed race. In
effect, the slate was wiped clean. The ancient world was destroyed, and a
new race slowly emerged. But we are still haunted by racial memories of
our planet's past. Every race and every culture has preserved guarded memories of that earlier epoch. Unfortunately, modern science has boxed itself
in and dedicated itself to proving Darwin's theory of evolution and other
theories that supply a rational, but not necessarily valid, explanation of
man's origin and past.

Chapter Six

A Funny Thing Happened
on the Way to Extinction

WANT TO DISCOVER A LOST CITY and be entered in the annals of archaeology? It's easy, according to James Randi, the famous magician and escape artist who has spent considerable time probing into the ruins of Asia and South America. Just visit an out-of-the-way place and ask the natives for directions to the nearest lost city, Randi explains. There are thousands of these structures on every continent, and only a comparative handful have been recognized by archaeology. Those prehistoric stonemasons were ubiquitous, and they left their works everywhere.

A young geologist named Karl Mauch found the lost city of Zimbabwe in southern Rhodesia in 1871 simply by asking an ivory trader for directions.* Mauch's story is filled with high adventure. The trader, a German-American named Adam Renders, rescued him from a tribe of hostile natives and led him to the site of the ancient ruins. Mauch decided Zimbabwe was actually the biblical gold center of Ophir, where the fruits of King Solomon's mines were collected. But all he and Renders found was a series of granite structures on top of a steep hill, filled with winding passageways and tunnels. The largest was the Elliptical Building, roughly 830 feet in circumference and 33 feet high. Nearby were two towers. A cave on a cliff some distance away has proven to have unusual acoustics. When someone speaks in the cave, his voice can be heard in the Elliptical Building but nowhere else.

---

*The whole country was renamed Zimbabwe when it gained independence from Great Britain in 1980.—ED.

"Doubtless, the native priests put this phenomenon to nefarious use," L. Sprague de Camp, a reformed science fiction writer, noted.

Archaeologists have been arguing about Zimbabwe for more than a hundred years. The ruins have been dated variously from A.D. 700 to 1500. They have been credited to everyone from the Phoenicians and the Egyptians to the naked Bantu tribesmen. Their workmanship is rather crude when compared with the far more impressive structures of Asia, the Pacific, and South America. Nevertheless, someone—we'll probably never know who—went to the trouble of dragging thousands of granite bricks to the top of a hill deep in the African jungle twelve hundred years ago and building an elaborate fortress-temple filled with labyrinths and passageways whose only apparent purpose is to drive archaeologists mad.

The city of Timbuktu was little more than a legend until the closing years of the nineteenth century, when French adventurers crossed two thousand miles of the Sahara wasteland and found it on the banks of the Niger River in what is now the country of Mali. It was settled in A.D. 1087 and was once a large, thriving trade center. Today it has a population of about eighty-five hundred.* The architecture of Timbuktu is not particularly impressive, and the city is most noted for the hundreds of storks who reside there.

Since a prominent city like Timbuktu could become "lost" in modern times, it is not surprising that even larger and more impressive cities, such as Angkor Wat, could get lost altogether. Angkor was only a myth until explorers stumbled onto it in Cambodia in 1857. It contains enormous temples and pyramid-like structures apparently related to the mysterious structures of the Pacific islands. The walls are covered with statues and bas-reliefs, and the origins of the city are lost in a welter of half-remembered legends. Local natives still speak of the great god-like beings who built the place. Hard facts are rare. One story popular soon after Angkor's discovery is that the city was abandoned suddenly (probably around A.D. 1300) in the same way that the

---

*Population figures for most parts of the world are debatable. The figures used in this book are up-to-date [as of 1971—ED.] estimates from the official statistics of the United Nations and sources such as the *Hammond World Atlas*.

Easter Islanders threw down their tools at their quarries and fled. At least it is obvious that Angkor was the product of an advanced culture of engineers and stonemasons and that their culture vanished rather suddenly.

History demonstrates that men have often built imposing, elaborate cities, flourished in them for hundreds or even thousands of years, then deserted them to live in simple grass huts on their perimeters. Wars and natural calamities often played a part in this pattern, of course. Great cultures have risen and then died out. Men returned to simpler ways of life. It is a natural order of things. A thousand years from now people may be living in thatched shacks in New Jersey and on Long Island within full view of the decaying towers of Manhattan. They may tell the children about the peculiar ancients who built the towers as part of the strange religion that worshiped the great god Money.

In the Middle East the little country of Jordan is filled with Roman ruins predating the Christian era. A large Roman theater with a seating capacity of four thousand can be found near Amman. There are great temples and triumphal arches and countless stone columns lining dead streets paved with large stone blocks.

Far to the south of Amman, in the midst of the unfriendly desert the traveler enters a narrow gorge that leads through the cliffs to an ancient city right out of the Arabian Nights. This is Petra, carved out of the red sandstone cliffs and filled with stately columns and temples. This Arab Shangri-la was constructed around 700 B.C. and must have housed thousands of people. Food, water, and supplies had to be brought in through the gorge—the only approach—from miles away. Thousands of men must have labored for generations, hacking these monuments out of the walls of this hidden valley. Some of the ruins are pre-Roman. There are ancient tombs, and a narrow stone staircase leads to an area on top of a cliff where two twenty-foot obelisks are located on "the high place"—a platform measuring forty-five by twenty feet. Perhaps Professor Agrest would regard it as another launching platform for nuclear rockets.

The culture that built Petra is lost in legend and archaeological confusion, but in the city's final days it was used as a hideout by desert bandits.

For the most part, believers in Mu, Atlantis, and flying saucers have ignored the ruins of the Middle East and Africa, concentrating instead on the lost cities of Central and South America. The fairly recent Mayan, Inca, and Aztec civilizations cannot account for all these ruins. There is evidence that another, possibly far more advanced, culture thrived in the Americas in earlier times. Remnants of that civilization may have been handed down to the Indians who followed.

Tiahuanaco, a fabulous stone ruin high in the Andes Mountains, has inspired more curiosity, speculation, and nonsense than any other. It has been the subject of countless books and articles and has been used to support the beliefs of nearly every outlandish cult going. In recent years there have been innumerable flying saucer sightings and appearances of little glowing green men around Lake Titicaca, which is 12,644 feet above sea level. Tiahuanaco is at the southeast end of the lake. Although the ruins cover only about one-sixth of a mile, they feature impressive *tumuli* (man-made mounds), a fifty-foot-high pyramid, and a number of stone platforms and underground chambers. The famous Gateway of the Sun is an arch weighing nearly ten tons. Archaeologists believe that the Tiahuanacans were part of an empire that preceded the Incas by two thousand years, but they left no written record, —and there are no local legends about them. When the Incas later conquered the Lake Titicaca region, they found Tiahuanaco abandoned.

While many of the structures in Petra were carved from the sandstone cliffs in place, some of the walls in Tiahuanaco were whittled out of huge blocks weighing as much as sixty tons and then somehow moved into place. Giant statues also stand around the site. One weighing twenty tons has been moved to a museum in La Paz. In their book, *The Great Idol of Tiahuanaco*, Hans Bellamy and P. Allan offer an interpretation of the symbols found on a huge statue discovered in a Tiahuanacan temple. They claimed the symbols recorded astronomical knowledge of a very advanced order.

Erich Von Däniken, author of *Chariots of the Gods*, visited the Andes in his search for evidence that spaceships had visited the earth in prehistoric times. He describes seeing a twenty-thousand-ton stone block near the ruins of the Incan fort of Sacsahuaman. Däniken explains:

It is a single stone block the size of a four-story house. It has been impecca-
bly dressed in the most craftsmanlike way; it has steps and ramps and is adorned
with spirals and holes…monstrous blocks stands on its head. So the steps run
downward from the roof; the holes point in different directions like the inden-
tations of a grenade; strange depressions, shaped rather like chairs, seem to
hang floating in space. Who can imagine that human hands and human endeavor
excavated, transported, and dressed this block? What power overturned it?
What titanic forces were at work here? And to what end?

The fortress of Sacsahuaman is surrounded by a wall sixty-feet high,
containing stones weighing as much as two hundred tons. *Two hundred tons!*
Morris K. Jessup, a qualified investigator, viewed the fortress and described
these stones.

All of them were crudely rough quarried and then ground into their desig-
nated niches in the structure by pushing them back and forth *in situ,* until they
fitted so closely, completely, and accurately that a knife blade cannot be inserted
between them. This is a logical and practical shortcut to effective stone fitting, which we have not equalled in modern engineering.

Science writer Joseph Goodavage questioned Jessup's theory in *Flying
Saucers—UFO Reports*, No. 4. The stones, he pointed out,

…had to be lifted into the air, placed roughly into their proper positions, and
then by some force inconceivable to us, shoved back and forth, grinding down
the roughly hewn surfaces until they fitted smoothly and perfectly into their
proper niches. To lift, swing into position, then rub the massive weight back
and forth (against enormous friction) without loosening its snugly fitting neighbors was no job for simple aborigines or even for an advanced Inca culture;
the fact is that Sacsahuaman was ancient long before the Incas appeared on
the scene.

To add to the mystery, some of the larger stones found in the Andes ruins
were quarried in a valley two hundred miles away. Somehow these enormous blocks of stone had to be transported up and down mountains to their

final resting place. Those fond archaeological inventions, wooden rollers and rafts, couldn't have been used. So how did the ancient builders accomplish this task?

A possible explanation taken seriously by some scientists and loudly berated by others is that these monuments were built in a time when the surface of the earth was actually different from what it is now. A time when the Andes were level with the rest of the land. Hans Schindler Bellamy prowled around Lake Titicaca and claimed that he found traces of marine sediment indicating that the Great Deluge had once engulfed the area. This of course was evidence that the ruins had been built before the deluge and were many thousands of years old.

Two Frenchmen, Louis Pauwels, editor of the magazine *Planète,* and Jacques Bergier, a nuclear physicist, seem to go along with Bellamy in their book, *The Morning of the Magicians.* They propose that the earth was once inhabited by a giant race that built the mounds and monoliths and maintained a worldwide civilization with key centers in the Andes, New Guinea, Mexico, Abyssinia, and Tibet. They were the true Atlanteans and were destroyed by some great cosmic disaster.

The evidence reviewed thus far does indicate that this planet was once occupied by a single great culture or a series of intertwining cultures that possessed secrets of engineering and stone building beyond anything known by the ancient Minoans, Romans, and Britons. They constructed their monuments in isolated places, such as the islands of northern Scotland, the Pacific, and the Andes Mountains, demonstrating an incredible sense of purpose as well as awesome perseverance.

Our anthropologists and archaeologists have been struggling to uncover and understand the history of the past four thousand years. They have steadfastly refused to consider the possibility that mankind may be only the latest race to infest the earth, that other races and other civilizations may have thrived here and died here. One of the increasingly popular themes in science fiction is the notion that an earlier superrace built spaceships and sent their members off to visit the stars. Now those space travelers are returning to home base in their flying saucers, and they're looking around in unhappy confusion, asking, "Where did everybody go? Who are all these pitiful little ants shooting at each other?"

Alfred Wegener, an obscure German meteorologist, died in 1930 after suffering fifteen years of ridicule, slander, and contempt at the hands of his peers and colleagues. He was branded a kook because he believed that the earth once contained two large land masses that had gradually split up and drifted apart to form the six continents. Every schoolboy who has ever studied a map of the globe has reached the same tentative conclusion, for the great land masses do seem to conform like the pieces of a massive jigsaw puzzle. Wegener's evidence was a bit more complicated than that, however. He considered fossils from different continents, climatic changes, and specific geological formations, such as mountains that seem to display marked similarities on the different continents. But science was not ready to consider the theory of continental drift in 1915. It was easier to denounce Wegener, dissect his ideas with more popular theories, and consign his books to the scrap heap. When Wegener died in 1930, his theory seemed to die with him.

In the late 1950s, the Wegener controversy long forgotten, a new crop of scientists began to explore the oceans, and new data was fed into computers. Mountain ranges were discovered under the oceans, laid out in ways that confirmed Wegener's earlier speculations. Almost overnight the continental drift theory became a new scientific fact. The National Science Foundation has now committed $5.4 million for new tests and studies. Alfred Wegener may soon have the last laugh.*

Rock layers at specific levels in South America have been found to match identical layers in Africa, indicating that both land masses were once a single unit. The current guess is that 150 to 200 million years ago there were two supercontinents. They broke apart and drifted away from each other slowly. They are still moving slowly, almost imperceptibly, and their move-

---

*See "The Confirmation of Continental Drift," Patrick M. Hurley, *Scientific American:* April 1968. Also, "Jigsaw of the Primeval World," *Life:* January 30, 1970.

ments have been measured by satellite photos and other means. North America is moving away from Europe at the rate of an inch per year.

New instruments are able to measure the magnetic fields of rocks on the ocean's bottom. These measurements indicate that the earth's magnetic field has frequently shifted, the North Pole becoming the South Pole and vice versa. Such magnetic shifts have occurred at least 171 times in the past seventy-six million years—further proof that the earth's crust is wriggling about.*

What all this means is that about two hundred million years ago during the age of the great reptiles—the Paleozoic Age—this was an entirely different planet. Perhaps it harbored life forms now unimaginable to us. Then it broke up, and new continents were formed, new climatic changes occurred, the physical environment itself may have changed. These changes could have brought about the sudden or gradual change of the life forms as they altered to adapt to the new conditions. Some of the puzzling erratics discussed in chapter 1 could have been produced by a form of intelligent life now lost and forgotten. But a lot of other changes can occur in two hundred million years. It is doubtful if even the most advanced civilization could produce any quantity of monuments and artifacts that could withstand millions of years of erosion and geological change.

The Atlantophiles are not too happy with the continental drift theory because it virtually excludes the possibility that any large land mass could have existed between North America and Europe. It might not rule out Mu or Lemuria, however. Other stubborn cultists are already leaping onto the continental drift bandwagon and claiming one of those two land masses as their favored lost continent.

Our flimsy knowledge of the very ancient past is based entirely upon the discovery and interpretation of fossils found in the various rock layers of the earth's crust. This inexact science called paleontology is only two hundred years old. We haven't dug deeply enough or studied things thoroughly

---

*See "Reversals of the Earth's Magnetic Field," Allan Cox, *Scientific American:* February 1967.

enough to reach reliable conclusions about the distant past. So many of the facts commonly accepted today are only educated guesses.

If the earth has suffered truly cataclysmic changes in the past two hundred million years, we must first know of and understand those changes completely before we can accurately assess the meanings of rock formations. It seems unlikely that we will ever be able to develop methods for collecting evidence that will give us conclusive truths about the earth's past. Astronomers and mineralogists were astounded and upset by the rocks our astronauts scooped up off the surface of the moon, because they indicated that the moon was four billion years old or even older, and it may be even older than the earth itself. Some astronomers had been pushing the theory that the moon was really just a chunk of the earth that had been scooped out of the Pacific Ocean area and tossed into space somehow. That theory and many others went down the drain when our first space module dropped onto the Sea of Tranquillity.

Geologists and paleontologists have developed reasonable evidence that the earth has passed through several glacial periods, or ice ages. These seem to be cyclic, with minor ice ages occurring every twelve thousand years or so and with major glacial periods taking place over longer periods. These ice ages suggest a really major catastrophe—a sudden shift of the earth's entire axis.

If you lived on the planet Uranus, the seventh planet from the sun, you would be exposed to a pseudo-ice age every 21.5 (earth) years. Our knowledge of Uranus is admittedly flimsy, and when and if we ever manage to visit it, we may find that many of the currently accepted facts about the planet are erroneous, just as our moon landings disproved many of the previously accepted facts about our own satellite. In any case, the best astronomical information indicates that Uranus has a very wobbly axis and that it flips over about four times for each of its circuits around the sun. (A Uranus year is eighty-four earth years.) A resident living on a fixed point on Uranus would find himself shifting drastically away from or toward the sun every 21.5 years. If the planet were closer to the sun, these shifts could produce dramatic changes of climate.

It is possible that the earth's orbital mechanics include similar fluctuations of the axis over longer periods. Scientists have figured out that there are minor climatic changes on earth every 170 years due to minor axis shifts. The magnetic polarity of our planet is quite unstable. The magnetic South Pole is not a fixed point but moves steadily in a two-hundred-mile circle. As already noted, the poles reverse themselves every few million years. Studies of the rock levels of the last Ice Age have produced evidence that major shifts of the earth's crust or the planet's entire axis occur every twelve thousand years or so. Such shifts would change the climate completely; frigid areas would suddenly be in the tropic zones, water would inundate land areas, and of course, all life would be affected. Seashells and fossils have been found in the heart of the Sahara desert, indicating that it was once covered with water.

In a stimulating article in the *Saturday Evening Post* of January 16, 1960, zoologist Ivan T. Sanderson documented the amazing results of one of these planetary inversions. Prehistoric mammoths found preserved in the frozen muck of Siberia had mouthfuls of unswallowed plants, as though they had been quick frozen while munching happily on their feeding grounds. Sanderson pointed out that the only way these animals could have been so splendidly preserved was to have been exposed to an incredible drop in temperature. This could have occurred in several ways, he pointed out cautiously. The earth's crust could have shifted very suddenly, carrying the animals farther north very rapidly, the entire axis could have rocked over, or some cloud of frigid gases from space could have suddenly engulfed the entire planet. Whatever the case, the discovery of these animal carcasses is solid evidence that some unexplained calamity took place with fierce suddenness thousands of years ago.

Decades earlier an Austrian mining engineer named Hans Hörbiger had developed a fanciful theory to explain the earth's early history. He envisioned huge spheres of ice crashing into the planet and talked of captive moons, which predate our present moon, entering retrograde orbits, their gravity tearing up our seas and reshaping the earth's surface. His eight-hundred-page *Glazial Kosmogonie*, published in 1913, enraged the astronomers and scientists of Germany and Austria. The late Willy Ley, the

German rocket authority and science writer, summed it up when he said, "To pick flaws in this theory is about as easy—and as pleasant—as gathering Japanese beetles from an infested flower bed."

But Hörbiger found a powerful ally, another Austrian named Adolf Hitler. In 1925, Hörbiger delivered this ultimatum to the scientific world:

> The time has come for you to choose—whether to be with us or against us. While Hitler is cleaning up politics, Hans Hörbiger will sweep out of the way the bogus sciences. The doctrine of eternal ice will be a sign of the regeneration of the German people. Beware! Come over to our side before it is too late!

Powerful backers materialized, and Hörbiger set up offices and recruiting campaigns for his doctrine of eternal ice—*Wel* (*Welteislehre*). His scientific critics were soon subjected to horrifying harassment and cringed in terror as *Wel* took on all the dimensions and power of a political party. Every good Nazi had to declare, "I swear that I believe in the doctrine of the eternal ice."

With the disintegration of Nazi Germany, *Wel* also seemed to melt away. But recently Hörbiger's concepts were resurrected by Pauwels and Bergier in *The Morning of the-Magicians*. "There have been four geological epochs," they state flatly, "because there have been four moons." The earlier epochs were influenced by gravitational changes and factors that produced giant animals and plants, "...and in a world peopled by monsters there appeared this first man of immense size bearing almost no resemblance to us and possessed of a different kind of intelligence." Cosmic rays became stronger in those days, they tell us, and produced a vulgar mutation. Survivors of this race of giants overlapped into the modern epoch and are mentioned in the folklore of many races, usually being described as evil and violent characters.

One of Hörbiger's disciples was Hans Bellamy, who sifted myth and legend to find further proof for the doctrine of eternal ice. It is not unusual that the *Wel* believers turned to the Atlantis literature and found in it some of the evidence they sought. The Atlantophiles had also scoured folklore and uncovered innumerable references to earlier global disasters.

Although scientists sneer at the use of myths as evidence, it is obvious that all the isolated races of mankind managed to preserve the same kind of stories. Of all the bits and pieces assembled from these ancient tales, the most common is the universal account of a great flood that occurred simultaneously over the entire planet (if the assorted legends have been dated correctly). Many Indian tribes in the Americas have myths about arks and Noah-like personalities who survived the flood. If we take these things at their face value, we can assume that the earth did experience a phenomenal rising of the waters in fairly recent times, that a large part of the land surfaces were inundated, and that some human beings escaped because *they had been warned* in advance and had fled to high places or had constructed ships that were sufficiently seaworthy to withstand the torrents.

The flood legends form the cornerstone of the Atlantis myth. A colorful politician named Ignatius Donnelly was responsible for the revival of interest in Atlantis in the late nineteenth century. He collected hundreds of fragments of archaeological erratics and wrote a number of bestselling books. He also managed to find time to serve as a U.S. congressman and state senator and even ran for vice president on the Populist ticket in 1901. Donnelly's *Atlantis: The Antediluvian World* is still in print and makes some sense, even though it fails to prove the existence of Atlantis. It does prove that other civilizations existed before the present epoch. Donnelly also advocated a theory claiming that a visiting comet had upset the balance of the earth in earlier times and produced catastrophic effects. Hörbiger carried the theory several steps further.

Comets have always served as a kind of scientific catchall. Although we actually know very little about these celestial objects (since we've never managed to catch one), astronomers like to believe that these fireballs are made of ice and that the huge chunks of ice that have crashed out of the sky for centuries were really from the tails of comets. In recent years many prominent scientists have seriously explained flying saucers as being the debris from comets' tails. During the UFO flap of 1966, the late Sen. Robert F. Kennedy sent out form letters stating that, "One explanation of this phenomenon connects the lights that are seen with the gaseous tails of comets."

If a comet ever did strike the earth, it might make life here rather uncomfortable. Scientists have estimated that if a solid meteorite only a mile in diameter should strike the planet intact, the impact and concussion could destroy a large part—or all—of life here. There are a number of large meteor craters, all very ancient, which prove that such collisions have taken place.

Ancient civilizations could have been destroyed by any one of these potential catastrophes, as well as such things as enormous earthquakes and volcanic eruptions. Our planet is really unstable. Mountains are always blowing up. The crust is constantly shifting, generating earthquakes that take a frightening toll in lives and property every year. Rivers overflow and floods occur with appalling regularity. Enigmatic fireballs can sweep down out of the sky suddenly and unexpectedly and burn up whole cities like Chicago.

On top of all these hazards, we have the most dangerous factor—man himself. He has made war an economic and political necessity. The ruins of the Middle East and Europe stand as testimony to his ability to destroy whole civilizations by himself without any outside help.

Among the traditions of the Hopi Indians is the story of *Kuskurza,* the third world or epoch, which lay "in the east" (Atlantis again!). They developed flying machines called *patuwvotas,* according to Frank Waters in his *Book of the Hopi*: "Some of them made a *patuwvota,* and with their creative power made it fly through the air. On this many of the people flew to a big city, attacked it, and returned so fast no one knew where they came from. Soon the people of many cities and countries were making *patuwvotas* and flying in them to attack one another. So corruption and war came to the Third World as it had to the others."

With present-day inflation, theories are the cheapest commodity around, costing less than a dime a gross. It is better to stick with the available facts. Those facts are that one or more civilizations preceded early man and left behind magnificent megaliths as proof of their artistic and engineering abilities. Something destroyed those civilizations, or perhaps they destroyed themselves. Great civilizations have risen and died within the past two thousand years alone. Our own civilization may be following the same unhappy route, and two thousand years from now the earth may again flip over on its axis. Great sheets of ice may bury the rubble of our cities. Silt and stones will wash over our towers and fortresses. And somewhere a handful of beings, reduced to savagery by necessity, will tell tales around their campfires about us and how we even dared to reach for the moon. Thousands of years after that, a new breed of anthropologist will collect those tales and scoff, even though all the tribes from all parts of the planet will have the same tales to tell. It is plainly impossible, those scientists will say, that any supercivilization could have existed in prehistoric times. And primitive man could hardly have flown to the moon. It is folly to even listen to such nonsense. It's far more fruitful to measure and study those giant faces carved into Mount Rushmore...faces that are obviously replicas of ancient gods. Probably they were carved by the same primitives who erected that great ring of stones in the British Isles, they will observe sagely.

Mankind is like a broken record repeating the same refrain over and over again.

Chapter Seven

Scientists in Collision

IN 1950, A NEW METEOR arced across the horizon, spewing a long trail of crisp ideas that left the scientific establishment sputtering in rage. The meteor was a book dealing with history, astronomy, and archaeology. It was written by a psychiatrist and published by a major Madison Avenue house. Science editors and book reviewers across the country greeted it with awe, comparing its author with Galileo, Newton, Darwin, and Einstein. The public responded by making the book a bestseller. It was titled *Worlds in Collision* and written by Dr. Immanuel Velikovsky.

Dr. Velikovsky tore at the delicate underpinnings of modern science, applying excessive scholarship to the problems of how the planets were formed and what forces may have wrought changes in the earth. Along the way he was obliged to invent new theories based upon the flimsy (by scientific standards) evidence of mythology. He dared to throw out some of science's most coveted concepts, substituting his own cosmology.

The explosion followed almost immediately. The biggest names in astronomy and physics organized and fulminated. They set out to destroy this upstart by flooding his publisher's office with vicious letters threatening to boycott the firm unless Velikovsky's book was withdrawn. Since the publisher also had a profitable sideline of textbooks and was heavily dependent upon the academic community for support, this ugly campaign had some effect. An assistant editor who had first suggested publishing the book was fired, and publication rights were turned over to another publisher who did not have a textbook business.

Leading scientists gave public lectures denouncing Velikovsky. The scientific journals were filled with critical anti-Velikovsky letters and articles. It was modern science's darkest hour. "There was a response which for intensity and hostility was unequaled in twentieth century scientific history," the *Los Angeles Times* later noted.

What triggered this emotional outburst? Velikovsky's main theme was that the planet Venus was really a comet hurled out of the planet Jupiter. It had brushed past the earth, he said, on its way into orbit around the sun and had been observed by all the existing races and recorded in their mythology.

Immanuel Velikovsky was born June 10, 1895, in Vitebsk, Russia. He studied medicine and law at some of Germany's best universities (he couldn't go to a Russian college because he was a Jew), received his medical degree in 1921, and settled in Palestine in 1924. He knew Freud personally and corresponded with the great man in the last years of his life. In 1939, Velikovsky and his family moved to New York, intending to stay only eight months. But he was already toying with his theories, and he spent the next nine years in libraries conducting the exhaustive research that finally resulted in *Worlds in Collision*.

He died quietly in Princeton, New Jersey, in 1979. He was more fortunate than Wegener and his continental drift theory in that Velikovsky lived to see his critics silenced and many of his seemingly far-out concepts confirmed.

Ever since the invention of the printing press, publishers have been flourishing on bestselling books covering the whole spectrum of pseudoscience. Volumes of profound nonsense, such as the works on pyramidology and Atlantis, have sold in amazing numbers generation after generation. Nearly every major publisher has books on astrology and flying saucers on his lists. A large part of the endless stream of theses, papers, and learned studies by establishment scientists have in time proven invalid and more crackpot than even the cultist literature. It was incredible that Velikovsky's contemporaries singled out his work—a book that had taken nine years of careful study and research—for their venom. In retrospect many of the anti-Velikovsky critiques read like the work of deranged lunatics who had not even bothered to read the book they were attempting to criticize. They were against the book simply because it propounded ideas that were contrary to the accepted theories of the day. They resented the fact that a psychiatrist dared to speculate on astronomy and archaeology. He was an intruder. Above all they resented the fact that his book was very well written (most scientists are miserable writers).

"If I had not been psychoanalytically trained, I would have had some harsh words to say to my critics," Dr. Velikovsky said loftily in the early 1950s.

Orthodox scientists have always sneered at the works of Charles Fort, an American humorist who published four books of oddities and scientific anomalies, primarily because Fort delighted in attacking the scientific establishment. Now they tried to lump Velikovsky together with Fort. Scientists and the untutored followers of scientism spent years denigrating Velikovsky and generating the legend that he was just another crackpot. The aging psychiatrist just ignored them and went on writing books expanding his central thesis.* In a rare attempt at self-defense,** he stated that he hoped that future generations of scientists would understand his work more clearly. He wrote off his contemporary critics, and this prompted Martin Gardner to observe in 1952 that:

> Dr. Velikovsky is an almost perfect textbook example of the pseudoscientist— self-taught in the subjects about which he does most of his speculation, working in total isolation from fellow scientists, motivated by a strong compulsion to defend dogmas held for other than scientific reasons, and with an unshakable conviction in the revolutionary value of his work and the blindness of his critics.

One of the favorite points of the anti-Velikovsky critics was that he relied upon ancient myths and traditions for his evidence. Actually, in *Worlds in Collision*, he devoted many pages to this problem. Since he was trying to reassemble events that transpired in prehistoric times (before the advent of written records), he was obliged to perform a comparative study of early

---

*Among these are: *Earth In Upheaval, Ages in Chaos,* and *Oedipus and Akhnaton.*
***Harper's:* June, 1951.

legends. He recognized that the problem of interpreting such material correctly was monumental.

"Traditions about upheavals and catastrophes, found among all peoples," he wrote, "are generally discredited because of the short-sighted belief that no forces could have shaped the world in the past that are not at work also at the present time, a belief that is the very foundation of modern geology and of the theory of evolution."

Those were fighting words to the scientific establishment. Velikovsky compounded his felony by suggesting that numerous events and catastrophes long accepted in religious lore as miracles and acts of God were in reality observations of astronomical phenomena that could be explained. This was totally unpalatable to the scientific community and to many others as well.

In 1950, the otherwise staid *American Journal of Science* ranted that Velikovsky's book was "best described as burlesque of both science and history." Seventeen years later *Yale Scientific Magazine* devoted an entire issue to vindicating the good doctor.

What had happened in those seventeen years? For one thing, the Old Guard had changed to a degree, and many bright young men had emerged, clutching their slide rules as they rode the tails of new man-made comets to Venus and Mars. For another, the stupefying and stultifying atmosphere of the McCarthy era of the early 1950s had ended. Professor Lloyd Motz of Columbia University scented the tide of change, and in a letter in *Harper's* in October 1963, he cautiously admitted, "I do not support Velikovsky's theory, but I do support his right to present his ideas and to have those ideas considered by responsible scholars and scientists as the creation of a serious and dedicated investigator and not the concoctions of a charlatan seeking notoriety..."

Scientists and professors live in the uncomfortable atmosphere of the academic rule, "publish or perish." They grind out interminable research papers and studies, not because they have something to say, but because their livelihood often depends upon their ability to put their names into print. This unfortunate system has spawned an army of men whose academic credentials are sound enough but who indulge in quasi-research. Some even manage to acquire a considerable reputation by publishing a steady stream of unread books. Professor Motz's remark about "the concoctions of a charlatan seeking notoriety" is revealing, because scientists are painfully aware of the many charlatans in their own midst who thrive on such notoriety. Over and over again in the past, leaders of the scientific community have proven mere charlatans or, at best, competent organizers and administrators, while their less notorious contemporaries made the real contributions to their field. This spills over, of course, into other fields, such as literary criticism, where a man will write a critical essay of a famous author, and then others will write critical essays of the original critique. Soon the little literary magazines are actually feeding upon themselves, and the professors are quarreling about their said famous author.

Velikovsky became the most prominent victim of this system. If he had written a book about psychiatry (his own field) or sex and sold a million copies, no one would have cared. But when he invaded the turf of others, presented unpopular ideas in a logical and successful manner, and got the book published...well, he had gone too far. To the scientists of the 1950s, he *had* to be a "charlatan seeking notoriety." Like Herr Hörbiger of another era, they chanted, "Either you believe in us, or you must be treated as an enemy."

A decade later, the main dish served at many a scientist's table was crow.

Astronomers were dead certain in 1950 that both Jupiter and Venus were elderly planets, and after much peering through their telescopes, they had constructed some fanciful facts about both bodies. These facts were taught, as usual, to generations of school students as the gospel. Assorted studies had "proven" that the surface temperature of Venus was somewhere between twenty-five and thirty degrees centigrade, making it a relatively cool planet and possibly an inhabitable one. Dr. Velikovsky's theory was that Venus was actually an ex-comet and had been in solar orbit for only thirty-four centuries. If he was right, the surface of Venus would have to be considerably hotter.

In 1962, Dr. Frank Drake and other radio astronomers turned their equipment on Venus and discovered that its temperature based upon its radio emissions was at least 600 degrees Fahrenheit, or 315 degrees Centigrade. Later the United States and the Soviet Union sent unmanned space probes to Venus and confirmed that it was a mighty hot place and that there might be some source of surface heat other than solar radiation. Venus is the second planet from the sun after Mercury. Even the side turned away from the sun radiates considerable heat. Another interesting discovery was that Venus rotates slowly in a retrograde—that is, clockwise—direction and has movements that are in sharp contrast to the other planets in the solar system.* "Maybe Venus was created apart from the other planets," scientists at the Goldstone Tracking Station muttered in 1962, "perhaps as a secondary solar explosion or perhaps in a collision of planets."

There were other factors, such as the heavy hydrocarbon atmosphere of the planet, which seemed to confirm Dr. Velikovsky's 1950 speculations. Venus is definitely an oddball among the planets, but the astronomers of 1950 didn't know any of this.

Turning to the ancient records for his evidence, Dr. Velikovsky pointed out that early peoples had recorded Venus as an exceptionally bright object trailing smoke. The Chinese, Mayas, Toltecs, and Aztecs also recorded its motion...and the early Venus apparently followed a much different orbit, or trajectory, than the diminished orb now visible in our skies.

The people of Mesopotamia did not even record Venus in their astronomical records. Later, the Chaldeans described it as a "bright torch of heaven" that "illuminates like the sun" and "fills the entire heaven." Other far-flung cultures preserved similar comments, all of which suggest that Venus began as a comet that roared very close to the earth at one point—close enough perhaps to cause tidal waves and spew burning fragments onto the earth's surface.

Another part of Dr. Velikovsky's evidence consisted of the stories of the "rain of fire" that encompassed the earth, and he quoted from Mexican texts as well as the records of the Assyrians. If he was right, then some of the oil deposits on earth were a result of that celestial shower. But geologists have always assumed that oil is created by a process that takes millions of years.

*"See Radar Observations of the Planets, " Irwin I. Shapiro, *Scientific American:* July, 1968.

Since *Worlds in Collision* was written, deposits of liquid hydrocarbons have been found and dated in the Gulf of Mexico and elsewhere, giving every indication that they are only a few thousand years old!

The ancient texts described the comet Venus as from the fifth planet, Jupiter. Was this possible? This was the flimsiest part of the Velikovsky theory, and the most widely attacked. Ironically, the very men who advocate the theory that tectites are the result of meteor impacts on the moon (chapter 4) are the same ones who deny that a Jovian comet could come into being, perhaps by the same process. Velikovsky proposed a collision of planets "as a possible source." The asteroid belt between Mars and Jupiter could be made up of surviving fragments from that awesome event. Our ideas about Jupiter itself have been revised considerably since 1950. We used to think of it as a gigantic planetary body composed of gases and liquids, but in recent years powerful radio waves have been detected coming from it. Apparently, there are great electrical storms on the surface, and some of these storms affect earthly radio waves as much, or more so, than sunspots. Studies of all this have led to a new theory, now quite popular among astronomers, that Jupiter may not be a planet at all. It may be a cold star. Maybe one planet could not give birth to another, but a star, even a cold star, could.

Jupiter's diameter is approximately eleven times the diameter of the earth, about eighty-six thousand miles. As nearly as we can determine, it revolves very rapidly on its axis; a Jovian day is less than ten earth hours long. Through the telescope it appears to be ringed with cloudlike bands, the most interesting feature of which is the famous red spot. This is an elliptical spot some forty thousand kilometers long and thirteen thousand kilometers wide—roughly equal in area to the entire surface of the earth. This spot was first observed by Robert Hooke in 1664. Astronomers have been watching it ever since. It also rotates with the planet but at different speeds. And it always remains in approximately the same latitude, wandering only slightly.

Morris K. Jessup and other ufologists have advanced the notion that the red spot is actually a great spaceship, a monumental ark from outer space, which transported the survivors of some dying world into our solar system. Some modern flying saucer contactees even claim that the spacemen have taken them to Jupiter and shown them this ark. Other contactees have been told stories about the ark by the spacemen. It is waiting for the day when the earth will be evacuated by the kindly space people. Then we will all fly off to the stars aboard it. Well, not all of us. Just those lucky humans who have been chosen by the space people. Several dry runs have already been held in recent years with the chosen contactees closing down their homes and businesses to sit on a hill or mountaintop and wait for the evacuation to begin. A number of these dry runs are documented in my book, *UFOs—Operation Trojan Horse*. Jupiter's ark is an integral part of modern flying saucer lore.

Stanley Kubrick's epic motion picture, *2001*, added to this lore by having astronauts head for Jupiter after a mysterious monolith was discovered on the moon. The monolith, a faceless gray slab, is used throughout the film as the symbol of some extraterrestrial force guiding man's destiny. In the closing scenes of the film, scenes that have thoroughly baffled many moviegoers, an astronaut arrives on Jupiter only to enter into a new phase of evolution: a kind of rebirth. Shorn of its cinematic mysticism, the film is a restatement of what many cultists have been saying all along.

The flying saucer buffs have been misled by astronomical terminology. Although the red spot is usually termed an "object," it could be almost anything. Bernard M. Peek, an amateur astronomer, called it a raft and suggested it could be some form of water floating like an iceberg in the Jovian atmosphere. Professor Raymond Hide of the British Meteorological Office proposed in *Scientific American* in February 1968 that it could be the visible part of a phenomenon known as a Taylor column—a stagnant cylinder of liquid centered above some depression or topographical feature on the planet below.

The late Frank Edwards, a radio news commentator and author of UFO books, poetically equated it with a giant eye always turned towards the earth. Some followers of Velikovsky have asserted that the red spot is really the hole left behind when Venus was catapulted out into space.

In order for a body the size of Venus, which is only slightly smaller than the earth, to be successfully hurtled out of Jupiter, it would have to attain an incredible escape velocity to overcome the great mass and gravity of the planet. Achieving this velocity would require a tremendous amount of energy, or as Professor Motz put it, "...to eject a planet like Venus, Jupiter would have had to release in a matter of seconds or minutes as much energy as the Sun emits in more than a year. Jupiter would therefore have appeared as bright as a nova [an exploding star], that is about a million times as luminous as the sun..."

Dr. Velikovsky attempted to explain this by theorizing that a large mass on a near collision course with Saturn and Jupiter may have set the cosmic machinery in motion.

Whatever may have happened, Velikovsky's main premise is that Venus is a young planet. He predicted in 1950 that Venus would prove to be hot and that it would display orbital eccentricities. These claims have now been verified. He claimed that the ancient records stand as proof that Venus was not even present in the skies until fairly recent times, that it first appeared as a comet hauling a tail and followed a course somewhat different from its present one. Its passage through our solar system caused massive disturbances on earth and probably wholesale destruction. There are written records of those disturbances and archaeological and geological evidence of that destruction.

In relatively recent times, Venus posed a new mystery. Today's astronomers agree that our sister planet has no moons. But a satellite was observed orbiting Venus in 1672 by a prominent astronomer named Cassini. He saw it again in 1686. Other well-known astronomers, using primitive but adequate instruments, sighted it in 1740, 1759, 1764, and 1791. They all noted that it seemed to be about one fourth the size of Venus itself (giving it a diameter of two thousand miles) and that it was very bright, almost luminous. It's very hard to lose something two thousand miles across...even in space. But no astronomer has seen this object since 1791. Flying saucer cultists have taken Venus' vanishing satellite to their bosom, claiming naturally that it was really a gigantic spacecraft. But the object's extreme luminosity could mean that it was a fragment of the Venus comet itself, following a retrograde orbit that eventually sent it into the planet's surface.

We have followed a long and bizarre trail from the ancient rumors of massive catastrophes to the Atlantis-bound theories of Donnelly to the Ice

Age notions of Hörbiger's *Wel* and finally to the carefully researched and thought-out conclusions of Dr. Immanuel Velikovsky and his still controversial concept of colliding worlds. These men and their many followers were probably mostly wrong...but there is always a chance that they might also be partially right. While their peers and colleagues have fumed, fussed, fought, ridiculed, and attacked their bold syntheses, a new generation of scientists has steadily uncovered substantial scientific evidence that seems to support them. New theorists will undoubtedly seize upon this new evidence and construct concepts that will make them seem pikers.

We are beginning to realize that the earth's crust is in constant motion, that the continents are adrift. The whole planet may flip-flop on its axis every few thousand years, causing water to bury land areas, bringing new land areas to the surface, and thrusting temperate zones into the Arctic cold to be smothered by ice. And if we can accept Velikovsky, our little mudball is running the constant hazard of encountering objects and forces in space that can wreak unbelievable havoc in hours or days. The moon could even fall on us one day, or the sun could suddenly explode. Our whole technological civilization could be wiped out in a flash.

It would not be too surprising, therefore, if other great civilizations might have flourished on this planet many thousands of years ago. Other great races, not necessarily linked to us biologically, could have existed here. The supergiants of Pauwels and Bergier could have been real. All that has survived of that ancient race are the puzzling stone monoliths and the great mounds and ridges. It was a logical step for a supercivilization to move from the construction of mounds and earthworks to the building of the more permanent pyramids of Egypt and South America. Their culture, or remnants of it, survived and was imitated by early man. For thousands of years superb stonemasons labored all over this planet, erecting pyramids, then temples, then great cities. Our sciences have timidly attempted to reconstruct the history of the past three or four thousand years, never daring to look beyond. And woe to anyone—such as Velikovsky—who does dare.

Part Two

If the religious projections of man correspond to a reality that is superhuman and supernatural, then it seems logical to look for traces of this reality in the projector himself.

—Peter L. Berger, *A Rumor of Angels*

Chapter Eight

Mimics of Man

THE ANIMAL WORLD is filled with incongruous redundancies. There are insects that resemble twigs and sticks, fish that look like harmless underwater plants, animals that appear to be rocks and ferns. Some nonpoisonous snakes imitate the coloring and appearance of their deadlier cousins. Numerous tasty insects discourage their enemies by imitating poisonous centipedes and scorpions. The animal and insect world is thronging with fakers and imitators and cunning masters of camouflage. One insect is so cleverly disguised that it can march along with formations of fierce army ants unnoticed. It even imitates the scent of the army ants.

Man, the most vicious and wanton killer of the animal world and the natural enemy of all wild things, has his imitators, too. Overt contacts between man and paraman have numbered in the millions throughout history. Legend and lore are rich with such incidents of contact. Our great religions are founded upon encounters with angels and demons. The annals of psychic phenomena are filled with accounts of seemingly chance meetings with these ultraterrestrials. Some of them seem dull and inconsequential and even easily explainable; others are witnessed by groups of reliable people and produce testimony that could have been written by a drunken science fiction author.

"Living among us undetected may be creatures (not necessarily alien) with all the outward appearances of human beings," ufologist Alex Saunders wrote in *Quest* magazine, October 1969. "The mimic would of necessity be a 'lone wolf,' likely living in a large, bustling city where the eccentric and the odd may flourish unhindered. For it is a curious fact of nature that that which is in plain view is often best hidden."

Another famous ufologist, Aimé Michel, has also commented on these mysterious mimics: "Certain cases have been checked and found to be perfectly authentic. But they are so absurd (because they are *mimetic*) that folk do not dare to talk about them. No useful research can ever be done so long as absurdity produces complexes in us."*

Early man was very aware of the existence of these mimics and tended to separate them into two groups: gods and demons. All religions have always warned their followers to be cautious of false angels and demigods. The Bible repeatedly discusses these entities and their influence upon man, always describing them as humanlike beings usually traveling in threes and possessing remarkable superhuman powers.

"Be not forgetful to entertain strangers, for thereby some have entertained angels unawares," we are warned in Hebrews 13:2.

Three men, usually of Oriental countenance and dressed in somber black clothing, play important roles in both flying saucer and religious lore. For years the flying saucer researchers who encountered these Men In Black (MIB) believed they were secret agents of the CIA sent to harass them. These MIB have been seen most often riding about in large black automobiles, usually Cadillacs, and they have engaged in frightening tactics, harassing amateur UFO sleuths. There are hundreds of reports from all over the world in which these mysterious gentlemen have approached UFO witnesses and investigators, warning, even threatening, them to be silent about what they had seen.

Since these entities and their big black automobiles have an uncanny talent for disappearing into thin air, investigators examining the stories of their victims have tended to dismiss such accounts as lies and hallucinations. Then, as has happened in so many cases, when these skeptical investigators had MIB encounters of their own, they have panicked in confusion. There has been an appalling number of sudden deaths, suicides, and nervous breakdowns among UFO investigators in the past twenty years.

On the religious level, these same MIB, answering the same descriptions of the UFO harassers, have always been regarded as agents of the devil—or

---

*The Humanoids, a special issue of Flying Saucer Review: London, England.

the devil himself. The antics of these characters have kept the devil myth alive into modern times, and there are still numerous religious cults hopelessly engaged in battling and trying to outwit them...but they always manage to stay one jump ahead of their pursuers. Most of their deeds and manipulations appear to be nothing more than mischievous games.

The activities of these parahumans are largely confined to specific areas of this planet, where they appear and reappear century after century. "The angels keep their ancient places," poet Francis Thompson wrote. Thus there are many "haunted" places all over the world, shunned by ancient man or made sacred by him. These are precise geographical locations, and anyone digging into the history and lore of such locations will find thousands of accounts of ghosts, demons, monsters, and flying saucers pinpointed within a few square miles and covering a thousand years or more of time. To UFO cultists such places are Windows: entry points for spaceships from some distant planet. Occultists teach that these are Gateways, weak spots in the earth's etheric envelope through which beings from other space-time continuums seep through into our reality.

Sussex County in England is one Gateway, as are the Mississippi Valley, the Ohio Valley, and parts of our Western states, such as the area around Prescott, Arizona. There are literally thousands of these weak spots all over our planet. Paranormal and supernatural activities in these areas seem to be controlled by complicated cyclic factors. Periodically, all hell breaks loose in all these places simultaneously, and then we have a flap, or wave, of UFO sightings, apparitions, poltergeists, sudden inexplicable disappearances of animals and human beings, mysterious fires, and even a form of mass madness.

Researchers are only now beginning to untangle the cycles involved. For some unknown reason a high proportion of all these activities seem to occur on Wednesdays and on the twenty-fourth of the month. This has been a stable factor throughout history. The biblical prophet Zachariah reported (Zachariah 1:7) an angelic visitation, "Upon the four and twentieth day of the eleventh month," circa 520 B.C. The most famous flying saucer sighting of modern times, that of private pilot Kenneth Arnold near Mount Rainier in Washington, occurred on June 24, 1947. Note that many of the events discussed throughout this book took place on the twenty-fourth of the month.

Paranormal events also seem to cluster around the tenth of the month. Early peoples were aware of these factors and linked them with the phases of the moon. They thought the full moon influenced human behavior and produced lunacy. Appearances of UFOs and assorted apparitions do seem to increase during specific periods of the lunar cycle, and as noted in chapter 2, the human mind does seem to be involved. Many of these things have been carelessly dismissed as hallucinations because *only certain people can see these things at certain times.* However, a great many factors are involved. Recent studies indicate that persons of high psychic potential, who experience prophetic dreams and flashes of extrasensory perception (ESP), are more prone to see these things than people with little or no psychic ability. Polls and tests conducted over the past century by assorted scientists indicate that about one-third of the population possesses active or latent psychic abilities. They constitute our main body of UFO witnesses. The other two-thirds have never had any personal experiences of this sort and so, naturally enough, dismiss all of this as utter rubbish.

Two independent statistical studies of available UFO reports were conducted in 1970 and confirmed that the highest number of UFO sightings took place on Wednesdays. An amateur group, the American Flying Saucer Investigating Committee of Columbus, Ohio, ran a study of 929 UFO reports from the year 1968 and found that Wednesdays produced the greatest number—152. A more elaborate professional computer study of 7,025 sightings from the years 1922 to 1969 was carried out by Dr. David Saunders of Colorado University. He too found that the greatest number of sightings (1,077) occurred on Wednesdays. The lowest number in the Ohio study was 117 for Sundays; the lowest number in the Saunders' study was 903 for Saturdays. Although these are only pilot studies and much more work along this line will be necessary before any definite conclusions can be reached, it is obvious that these things are not random and sporadic but are governed by a definite time cycle of some sort. Factors of coincidence, innocent errors, misinterpretations of ordinary aircraft and mundane natural phenomena, weather balloons, and so on must be filtered out.

Another computer study of twelve hundred anomalies and unusual occurrences, sifted from the works of Charles Fort, was recently carried out by C. L. Mallows of the Bell Telephone Laboratories. Here it was found that a broader cycle of 9.6 years was seemingly involved. "The conclusion is inescapable that these cycles of activity, which pass through our world like radio waves of enormous length, must have a common cause," Damon Knight explained in his book, *Charles Fort: Prophet of the Unexplained.* "The cause of the cycles, the controlling force that keeps them in synchrony, must lie outside the earth."

The Bell study includes such diversified phenomena as sky falls (odd objects dropping out of the sky, unusual storms, rains of frogs, etc.), things observed in space, and things seen in the sky. All of these phenomena tended to cluster—to occur simultaneously in specific months and specific years. The waves or cycles of these events were repeated approximately every 9.6 years. The study dealt largely with data from the nineteenth century.

Ancient magicians and seers were quite familiar with these cyclic factors. The earliest religious and occult lore discusses rays that periodically sweep our planet from some extraterrestrial source and cause everything from miracles to madness and catastrophes. Strangely, the Australian Aborigines, the South American Indians, and the tribes of Africa, as well as the ancient Babylonians and other early cultures, *all* pinpointed the Pleiades (a cluster of seven stars), and the constellation of Orion, as that source of these rays. Rays from outer space are an integral part of all human folklore.

In time all of these intangibles will be pinned down by courageous scientific investigators (studies of this kind are still very unpopular among scientists). Already we know (or have relearned) that all paranormal manifestations have a tendency to occur in the same places year after year; that they follow specific patterns within our own time scale; that only specific people can witness or become involved in these events. The logical jumping off place for future investigation is to study the witnesses in depth and to explore these Gateways carefully and methodically. Small groups of psychiatrists, parapsychologists, geologists, and physicists are now engaged in studies of this type.

One significant factor, which is hardly a secret to the occultists, is that the Window areas tend to be places where peculiar magnetic faults exist. Our haunted planet is covered with magnetic faults, and interestingly enough, many of them are grouped around the ancient mounds, temple sites, and spots where flying saucers are seen most frequently. Psychically oriented people living in these regions tend to have extraordinary experiences with elementals, angels, MIB, and spacemen (numerous examples will be given further on).

A leading authority on mythology and mysticism, poet Robert Graves, wrote: "There are some sacred places made so by the radiation created by magnetic ores. My village, for example, is a kind of natural amphitheater enclosed by mountains containing iron ore, which makes a magnetic field. Most holy places in the world—holy not by some accident, like a hero dying or being born there—are of this sort. Delphi was a heavily charged holy place."

Back in the Middle Ages the Vatican pointedly ordered that new churches should be constructed on the sites of old temples whenever possible. The tradition of sacred places runs deep and seems to be largely based upon the continuous observations of paranormal manifestations. The entities who allegedly approached human beings in miraculous events frequently ordered a church or temple to be built on the spot. But we didn't need an order to erect the great churches at Lourdes and Fatima after the entities appeared there. Remember the legendary nineteen-year cycle of Stonehenge, when the god was supposed to appear? Multiply the Fortean cycle of 9.6 years by 2.

A magnetic survey of the United States was carried out by the government in the 1950s. Maps detailing magnetic variations in nearly every state can be obtained from the Office of Geological Survey in Washington. Comparisons of the concentrations of paranormal manifestations with these maps show unique clusters around the magnetic aberrations. Could it be that periodic sweeps of those rays from outer space set up some kind of physical or psychic reactions in these fault areas? This is a question that could be answered scientifically, if only someone would put up the money, equipment, and personnel to make a study.

We are only reobserving the things that awed early man and inspired his superstitions and beliefs. Electromagnetic energy plays a key role in these manifestations. We are still learning about it. Our planet may be constantly interchanging energy with some outside force. This exchange of energy is an important part of occult belief. It occurs, we are told, on every level. Chinese philosophers of long ago contended that man was moon food (i.e., the energy of individual souls was drained off and absorbed by some extraterrestrial force that needed such energy to replenish itself). Later, theologians extended this to form the classic explanation that we were the subjects of a war between God and the devil...a war to win the souls of man and thereby control the planet. Thus, the demons and MIB who appeared in earlier times were supposed to have been after souls. They made lavish promises, according to the records, and offered fanciful philosophies and cosmologies, but as Swedenborg figured out, they always proved to be nothing but splendid liars.

Early investigators and thinkers soon realized they were dealing with magical beings who could imitate man and his works. Instead of being solid, physically stable assemblages of cells and matter, these entities are apparently temporary manipulations of energy. So the word "transmogrification" was used to describe them. These transmogrifications, according to the lore, could assume any form...from a wolf to a cat to a house, ship, or iridescent god of awesome proportions. They could appear clothed in rags or in gold crowns and expensive velvet robes. Worst of all, they had a penchant for playing all kinds of games with us, manipulating our fears and beliefs and even conning us into going to war against each other.

One alarming facet of their countless messages to percipients and contactees is their preoccupation with spreading racist propaganda. The messages recorded throughout history are filled with such propaganda. If the percipient was an Indian, the propaganda was aimed at a nearby tribe. If he was Hindu, it was directed at the Moslems. The elementals are purveyors of hate, and perhaps much of the racial prejudice blighting the human race was originally the product of their teachings.

Even those wonderful space people and Brothers from other planets manage to play this game. Long John Nebel, a New York radio personality, spent thousands of hours interviewing contactees and UFO buffs on the air over WNBC, and in his book, *Way Out World*, he offered this comment:

> A bit that has always bugged me is the racist propaganda which keeps cropping up from one group to another. In this area, regrettably, I'm unable to name names and cite occasions, since the allusions are always so carefully phrased so that the offenders could easily deny the intentions of their remarks. But the meaning is there, never doubt it. As is usually the case, the unfavored parties racially speaking are the Jews and Negroes, and the themes of both Fascism and Communism seem to echo from behind the scenes on more than a few occasion. But it's all part of the action.

Some contactees who claim to have visited Mars blandly point out that the planet is divided into zones with the Negro and Jewish Martians carefully segregated from the others. Even contactees of liberal persuasions repeat with some dismay the nastily racist remarks of the Venusians. The Jews are a favorite target of this outer space propaganda, as if they haven't got enough trouble already.

Until the past five or six years racial prejudice was actually a basic part of all the Western religions. After digging down to the source of these racist beliefs, there are always the ancient teachings of dubious messengers. They have kept the human race stirred up and at each other's throats for thousands of years. Now finally the Catholics are beginning to soften their traditional anti-Semitism, and the Mormons are beginning to face the fact that Negroes are also human beings.

Aside from their inveterate racism, the mimics are also fond of exploiting tense political situations. A band of phantom Indians plagued the settlers of Gloucester, Massachusetts, back in 1692. They appeared night after night, skirmishing with the English and firing bulletless guns. Although the Indians never killed or scalped anyone, the colonists were understandably upset and heavily fortified their positions. "The English became convinced that they were not real Indians," Sir Walter Scott reported, "but that the devil and his agents had assumed such an appearance."

The North American Indians have innumerable legends about an entity they called the Trickster because he would turn up occasionally and play wild and vicious pranks.

Earth's phantom inhabitants play many other roles, especially in the widely accepted sphere of psychic phenomena. Telly Savalas, the famous character actor, told Hollywood reporter Dick Kleiner a weird story involving a black Cadillac. It happened when Savalas was young and flat broke. His car ran out of gas on Long Island, and after he started walking, a black Cadillac "seemed to appear from nowhere," and the driver offered him a lift. The driver was dressed entirely in white—a refreshing switch—and said very little. But at one point he offered Savalas a dollar to buy some gas. The actor insisted that the man write down his name and address on a slip of paper so he could be repaid. They found a gas station, and the driver waited while Savalas bought a can of gasoline. Then they drove back to his own car in silence.

"I know Harry Agannis," the driver said suddenly. Savalas asked who Henry Agannis was. "He's a utility infielder on the Boston Red Sox," the man answered. That was the end of the conversation.

The man waited while Savalas poured the gasoline into the car, gave him a push to get him started, and then drove off with a wave. The next day Savalas was shaken by newspaper headlines announcing the sudden death of Harry Agannis. He decided to call the phone number on the slip of paper given to him by the man in the white suit. It was in Massachusetts, and a woman answered. Savalas told her he wanted to speak to Bill, the name on the paper. There was a pause, and another woman came on the line.

"I just met Bill last night," Savalas began, "and something happened, and I wanted—"

"You met him last night?" she interrupted, choking on sudden tears. Then she told him that her husband Bill had been dead for three years. Later she met with Savalas in New York and told him that her husband had been buried in a white suit. She showed him the last letter her husband had written, and he was startled to see that the handwriting exactly matched the handwriting on the slip of paper given him by the Cadillac driver.

The whole fabric of psychic belief is woven from such stories, which number in the many thousands and are accepted by millions as proof of survival after death. But investigators informed in the antics of the ultraterrestrial mimics are obliged to look deeper. These entities labor to cultivate belief in various frames of reference, and then they deliberately create new manifestations that support those beliefs. Savalas rode in a physically real Cadillac and spoke with a seemingly real man. If the incident was only a joke of some kind, it was a very complicated and pointless one.

Phantom campers, vehicles with built-on trailers, have been widely reported in the Western states in recent years. And we have reports of phantom airplanes and helicopters by the hundreds. In the 1930s thousands of people in northern Europe saw formations of mysterious airplanes over Norway, Sweden, and Finland. Despite extensive searches by the military forces of several countries, the source of these ghost flyers, as they were called, was never determined.* During World War II military intelligence groups collected a number of phantom airplane sightings from pilots returning from missions. Crews of several bombers from the Ninety-Second Group reported the following over Germany:

> Four P-47s, thought to be friendly American aircraft flown by the enemy, were observed on the approach to the Initial Point at 22,000 feet, heading 120° magnetic. These aircraft flew out to the side and parallel with the combat wing formation in the manner of fighter escort. They suddenly executed a 90° turn in toward the head of the combat wing formation. These aircraft were originally at eight hundred yards on the port beam. They approached to three hundred yards, when they nosed up and away, showing a full-plan view of themselves. *Positive identification is claimed.* The aircraft had brown fuselages, and the wings were a very dark color, almost black. No white cowling and no white tail markings were observed. No insignia was observed, and the

---

*For a full account of this interesting sequence of events see John A. Keel's *UFOs—Operation Trojan Horse.*

aircraft did not open fire. Several B-17s fired on them. The last P-47 escort had long since departed, and the enemy aircraft had been attacking for some time at this point.

The opening theory expressed in this intelligence report—"Four P-47s, thought to be friendly American aircraft flown by the enemy"—was proven invalid. The mystery planes did not fire at the American bombers, but were fired on instead. If the Germans had attempted such a ploy with captured aircraft, they certainly would have painted appropriate insignia on the planes. And after having succeeded in getting within three hundred yards of the bombers (which is very close), the pilots, if they were German, would certainly have opened fire. Instead, they scooted away, never to be seen again.

Low-flying mystery airplanes reported in 1969–70 were most often described as resembling P-38s, the twin-engined, dual-fuselaged fighters used in the Pacific in World War II. They were fast, noisy aircraft, but our mystery planes move very slowly and in complete silence. They execute impossible maneuvers, such as sudden right-angle turns, and disappear as mysteriously as they came. Only a handful of P-38s are still operational, and they are not the culprits in these cases. Like the ghost flyers of 1934, they are a dull gray and violate all regulations by failing to show any license numbers or insignia.

Could these phantom aircraft be part and parcel of the same phenomena that produce phantom automobiles and campers? Could they also be apparitions and transmogrifications of energy that can be properly categorized with the disappearing Indians of Gloucester? The evidence suggests that this could very well be the case.

In other ages flying ships were sometimes reported. England's scholarly *Flying Saucer Review,* May-June 1970, reprinted a fascinating story from 1743. A farmer near Peibo, Wales, claimed he had seen a flying sailboat that year. He estimated that it was about 1,500 feet in the air and could have been about ninety tons. The keel of the ship was clearly seen (thus ruling out mirages of ships far out at sea). Similar phenomena had been reported in the same area about ten years previous.

Fairy lore is also filled with alleged sightings of fairy ships complete with billowing sails.

Our problem is compounded by these amazing, confusing, and alas, scientifically inadmissible, subjective observations. The UFO cults have solved this dilemma by simply throwing out this kind of material and concentrating only on those reports that describe circular or cigar-shaped objects. We must, however, consider all the forms reported with equal care if we are to arrive at any valid conclusions.

There is no way to investigate a flying saucer after it has flown. But it *is* possible to study the people who saw it and the terrain over which it appeared. If we are dealing with clever mimics and transmogrifications of energy and if man has been observing these things throughout his history, then the real clues may be found in the thousands of volumes in all languages describing those observations and encounters.

One basic fact should be obvious from the foregoing: these entities and things are not necessarily from some other planet. They are actually closely tied to the human race, are a part of our immediate environment in some unfathomable fashion, and to a very large extent are primarily concerned with misleading us, misinforming us, and playing games with us. These mysterious members of the Wellsian Wings Over the World are our benefactors and our enemies. They educate us and they torment us. They have given us hope, guided our religions and philosophies, and watched us crawl out of the caves and build rockets to the moon.

They may have watched other civilizations come and go. They may have sincerely helped us to preserve the memories of those lost ages and those past mistakes. Or it all may be rubbish, and we may be nothing more than the pawns with which they play their mischievous games. Theologians and philosophers have always been troubled by the nearly impossible task of sorting the real from the unreal, the truth from the false. Perhaps the only workable criterion is the ancient one of judging them by their works.

Chapter Nine

Men-in-Black Lore and the CIA

"THERE IS NO TRUTH to the rumors that the flying saucers are from Spain, or that they are piloted by Spaniards," Gen. Carl Spaatz, Air Force Chief of Staff, told a press conference in 1948. This was an astonishing statement, since a review of all the UFO literature and the fan magazines of the period has failed to uncover such a rumor. It suggests that people must have been reporting slight, dark-complexioned pilots to the Air Force back in 1948, long before the UFO buffs started taking flying saucer occupant sightings seriously.

In his detailed report on the Maury Island UFO "hoax" of 1947, Kenneth Arnold also describes meeting a small, dark, foreign-looking man who was tinkering with the motor on a beat-up boat in Tacoma harbor. Ray Palmer, editor of *Amazing Stories* in Chicago, had commissioned Arnold to investigate the puzzling Maury Island affair, which began when a "donut-shaped object" had rained "slag" onto a boat near Maury Island. Pieces of that slag had killed a dog aboard the boat and slightly injured a boy, the son of Harold Dahl, who was piloting it. Early the next morning, according to Dahl's story, a 1947 Buick drove up to his home and a black-suited man of medium height visited him. This man, Dahl said, recited in detail everything that had happened the day before *as if he had been there.* Then he warned Dahl not to discuss his sighting with anyone, hinting that if he did there might be unpleasant repercussions that would affect him and his family. Since Dahl and the others had not yet told anyone of their sighting and since UFOs were still publicly unknown (Arnold's sighting over Mount Rainier and the attendant publicity did not occur until three days later), Dahl was naturally nonplussed by his strange visitor. This was the first modern MIB report.

Dahl's boss, Fred L. Crisman (he also owned the boat), became a central figure in the mystery. Dahl himself vanished soon after his interview with Arnold, and efforts by later investigators (such as Harold Wilkins, a British author) failed to locate him. Crisman had been a flier in World War II, and he was suddenly recalled into the service in 1947, flown to Alaska, and later stationed in Greenland. In recent years the amateur sleuths engaged in investigating the alleged conspiracy to assassinate President John F. Kennedy have tried to implicate Crisman. District Attorney James Garrison of New Orleans subpoenaed one Fred Lee Crisman of Tacoma, Washington, to testify before the grand jury listening to Garrison's evidence against Clay Shaw, according to wire service stories in November 1968. Crisman was identified as a radio announcer, but Garrison's investigators implied that he was either a member of the CIA or had been "engaged in undercover activity for a part of the industrial warfare complex." He allegedly operated under a cover as a preacher and was "engaged in work to help Gypsies." These stories caused a chain reaction in UFO circles, since UFO believers have long accused the CIA of being somehow connected with the flying saucer mystery. Of course, the CIA was in its infancy in 1947 at the time of the Maury Island case and was then largely staffed by naval personnel from World War II intelligence units.

Clay Shaw was tried early in 1969, accused by Garrison of having conspired to murder President Kennedy. He was found innocent and freed. The exact nature of Crisman's testimony before the grand jury is not known. He did not testify at the actual trial.

When Ray Palmer, one of the best-informed ufologists extant, summarized his own theories about the Maury Island mystery in the book he coauthored with Arnold, *The Coming of the Saucers*, he asked pointedly, "Was the Tacoma affair a hoax? Whose?"

In recent years many seemingly solid flying saucer cases have dissolved in confusion under close investigation. Often they appear to be outrageous hoaxes perpetrated by some mysterious third party, although the general tendency is to blame the innocent witnesses. These bizarre hoaxes are often identical to the mischievous fairy hoaxes and games of an earlier epoch.

The Maury Island case fell apart in Arnold's hands. The slag samples given to him by Dahl and Crisman were switched by someone; two investigating Air Force officers, Brown and Davidson, were killed when their plane crashed shortly after leaving Tacoma; Dahl vanished; Crisman was literally exiled to Greenland for two years; Tacoma newsman Paul Lanoe, who helped Arnold in his investigation, died suddenly a short time later. Palmer claims that a cigar box filled with original slag samples was stolen from his Chicago office soon afterwards.

At one point, Ted Morello of the United Press took Arnold aside and told him:

> You're involved in something that is beyond our power here to find out anything about…We tried to find out information at McChord Field [the Tacoma Air Force base] and drew a blank, and we have informants there who practically smell the runways for news…We've exhausted every avenue attempting to piece what has happened together so it makes some sense…I'm just going to give you some sound advice. Get out of this town until whatever it is blows over.

Arnold got into his private plane and headed for home. He stopped in Pendleton, Oregon, to refuel, and shortly after he took off again, his engine stopped cold. Only quick thinking and expert flying saved him from a serious crash.

Despite the statements of General Spaatz and Kenneth Arnold in 1947–48, slight, dark-skinned men did not really begin to appear in *published* UFO reports until around 1954. (There were, however, descriptions of dark—or heavily suntanned—UFO occupants as far back as 1897.) The Men in Black phenomenon did not really grip the UFO field until the early 1950s.

A pioneer ufologist, Albert K. Bender of Bridgeport, Connecticut, gave the MIB mystery new impetus when he suddenly closed down his International Flying Saucer Bureau in 1953, vaguely hinting that three men in black suits had terrorized him into abandoning his research. Other UFO researchers studied his guarded remarks and concluded that he had been pressured out of business by sinister agents of the government. Three years later Gray Barker, a UFO investigator in West Virginia, published *They Knew Too Much about Flying Saucers*, a book that dealt with numerous MIB stories from as far away as New Zealand. The Bender case was the cornerstone of Barker's theory that the MIB either represented some governmental authority employing "questionable methods" to "silence" UFO researchers, or that a more "fantastic sponsorship is responsible for their deeds." Many of these dark-skinned, Oriental-featured gentlemen visited UFO witnesses wearing Air Force uniforms. This fact and the vast quantity of reported visits quickly led the UFO buffs to believe that their enemy was indeed the U.S. Air Force. Soon the UFO believers and their organizations were devoting most of their time, energy, and money to investigating the Air Force and, as the paranoia mounted, to investigating each other. The popular books of Donald E. Keyhoe, a retired Marine Corps pilot, were largely concerned with the alleged Air Force and governmental conspiracy to hide the truth about flying saucers from the public. Other UFO writers of the late 1950s followed Keyhoe's example, and this monumental conspiracy became one of the main "facts" of ufology.

Ten years after he suddenly withdrew from UFO research, Albert K. Bender released his full story, *Flying Saucers and the Three Men*, which was privately published by Gray Barker. It proved to be far more unbelievable than any speculations. He claimed that he had been visited by dark-skinned gentlemen with glowing eyes who materialized and dematerialized in his apartment. On one occasion, he said, he had been transported to a secret UFO base in Antarctica, where he had been told the secret. The UFOs were here to collect a rare and valuable element from the earth's oceans. The project would be completed in the early 1960s, he was told, and then the flying saucers would leave our planet and he would be free to write about his experiences.

Bender's revelations made no sense to the UFO coterie, since few of them were acquainted with demonology and the fairy myths of the Middle Ages. They did not realize that his purported experiences followed classic patterns. In addition to his interest in flying saucers, Bender had also been involved in a study of black magic, and black magic, as we shall soon see, has always been a major method for conjuring up elementals. He had been plagued by odors of sulfur and strange poltergeistic manifestations during the period of the visitations. He also suffered certain medical effects, such as chronic headaches and lapses of memory, which are common symptoms of the contactee syndrome. The UFO buffs quickly branded Bender a nut who was trying to get rich from flying saucers (actually, his book sold only a few thousand copies to the UFO hardcore and made him the subject of considerable criticism and ridicule).

Countless MIB-type stories have now been collected and published by UFO investigators all over the world. Even the stuffy anti-UFO report of Colorado University, a study which had been commissioned by the Air Force in 1967, discussed a few cases. Case Number 52 of the report occupies eighteen pages and discusses in detail the strange experiences of a Santa Ana, California, highway inspector named Rex Heflin who took a series of Polaroid photographs of a circular object near a Marine Corps air field on August 3, 1965. He had copies made of these pictures, fortunately, and turned over the originals to two men who claimed to represent the North American Air Defense Command (NORAD). Later, NORAD officials emphatically denied that any of their personnel had visited Heflin, and the original photos have never been located.

Two years later, soon after scientists from Colorado University began their investigation of the Heflin case, he received another group of strange visitors. They appeared at his home at dusk on Wednesday, October 11, 1967, dressed in Air Force uniforms. Because of his earlier experience, Heflin inspected their credentials carefully and wrote down their names and other information. They questioned him about the photos and asked him if he knew anything about the Bermuda Triangle area where many planes and ships have vanished. "During the questioning, the witness says he noted a car parked in the street with indistinct lettering on the front door," the Colorado report states. "In the back seat could be seen a figure and violet (not blue) glow, which the witness attributed to instrument dials. He believed he was being photographed or recorded. In the meantime his FM multiplex radio was playing in the living room and during the questioning it made several loud audible pops."

Dr. James E. McDonald, a meteorologist from the University of Arizona, and other investigators later tried to check out the identity of these visitors. Again, they drew a complete blank. Despite their credentials and uniforms, these men were apparently impostors. Numerous other witnesses have also reported visits from men in big black cars, usually Cadillacs, with peculiar purplish glows lighting their interiors. There are even a number of witnesses who claim to have been temporarily kidnapped in such automobiles. They have described strange psychedelic lights on the dashboards which caused them to fall into hypnotic trances.

Some of these phantom vehicles have a special insignia printed on their doors—a triangle with a bolt of lightning passing through it. In other cases witnesses said the symbol was the classic triangle with an eye—the ancient symbol for the deity—and the MIB identified themselves as "agents for the Nation of the Third Eye." Such stories are rarely given wide circulation and are almost never published. So it is quite interesting that so many far-flung witnesses manage to come up with the same identical details.

One of the first clues that a UFO flap was about to break on Long Island in the spring of 1967 was a series of random reports describing strange Oriental or Gypsy-like entities parading across people's lawns in the middle of the night. One man living on an isolated farm near Melville, New York, said he saw a metallic disk hovering a few feet above one of his fields in broad daylight. A ladder was hanging down from it, he said, and as he watched, it was retracted into the object, and the whole thing flew off soundlessly. A few days later, he answered a knock on his door and was surprised to see a Gypsy lady standing there. She was dressed in a long gray gown and wore sandals. Her skin was a deep olive, and her eyes had an Oriental cast. She was about five feet, four inches tall, and her hair was long and "so black that it looked dyed."

"I have traveled a long way," she said in a low, accented voice. "May I have a glass of water? I must take a pill."

He gave her the water, and she took a round, green pill, thanked him, and left. He was puzzled that there was no car in sight. He lived on an isolated back road, and visitors, especially visitors traveling by foot, are very rare.

"I have traveled a long way" is an old Masonic pass phrase and is frequently used in these contacts. Sometimes the simple phrase, "What time is it?" or "What is your time?" is substituted. The pill-taking ploy is also a common procedure. When a most peculiar being visited a family on Cape May, New Jersey, early in 1961, he also took a pill. He too had "traveled a long way," and after conducting an inane interview with the family, he stepped into the night, got into a black Cadillac, and drove off with the lights out. A full summary of this case was published in *Flying Saucer Review*'s second special issue.

A woman living in an old house on the summit of a high hill in the Melville, New York, area had a visit from a strange quartet around the same time that the Gypsy lady dropped in on the farmer. Four Indians appeared on her doorstep after a heavy seasonal rainfall. Three of them were stately, dark skinned, with pointed faces and Oriental features. They were dressed in expensively cut gray suits. The fourth man looked different, more normal, she said, and was poorly dressed in a frayed black jacket.

They told her that their tribe had originally owned her property, and they were going to try to get it back. What frightened the woman most—and she *was* frightened, she admitted later—was that there was no mud on their neatly shined shoes and they had no car in sight. The road and her lawn were soupy with mud at the time. After they left, she realized they had left no footprints on her lawn.

In case after case, amateur UFO investigators have rejected the testimony of sincere witnesses who claimed to have seen UFOs land and entities dismount, because no footprints could be found on the site afterwards.

At 1:30 A.M. on Wednesday, March 1, 1967, a man named Dewitt Baldwin was hunting near Eden, New York, when, according to his story, he heard a funny noise and saw a circular, gold-colored object land.

"I was scared. I didn't know what to do," Baldwin said. "While I was watching it, a door opened—like a sliding elevator door—and a man walked out and down the incline of the machine. He was dressed in a sort of black tight-fitting suit like a flier and had on some sort of helmet and goggles.

"He asked me what I was doing. He wasn't white, and he wasn't a Negro. He talked very plainly with no accent. I told him I was hunting. He asked me if I was born here, and I said no, that I was born in Georgia. He took my gun, looked at it, and handed it back to me. He told me he would be back, walked up the saucer, got in, and seconds later zipped out of sight."

Mr. Baldwin found a crack in the muzzle of his shotgun after the man had examined it. Neither the object or the pilot left any marks in the fresh snow. Local UFO investigators regarded this as proof that Mr. Baldwin had fabricated his story and was merely seeking notoriety.

An Iowa college professor who writes popular books under the pseudonym of Brad Steiger has been investigating Men in Black cases in the Midwest for several years. In his book *Flying Saucer Invasion,* he disclosed another common MIB tactic which is being widely employed these days to discredit investigators. Steiger wrote:

> In the summer of 1968, Brad Steiger received a long distance telephone call from a journalist friend who was covering a UFO flap for his local newspaper. [Steiger wrote in the third person.] "Blast Brad Steiger and Joan Whitenour [a Florida researcher who collaborated with Steiger] and down with John Keel!" he thundered.
>
> Steiger, recognizing his friend's voice, asked him what the trouble was.
>
> "I'm trying to cover this flap over here—my lord! Everyone has seen these UFOs!—but every time I try to dig deep, the eyewitness clams up and says. 'I won't say more. Brad Steiger says awful things will happen to me if I tell too much.' One lady said that John Keel had told her that she would be carried off by the saucer people if she talked to anyone about her sighting."
>
> Steiger knew that neither he nor Keel were in that particular area at that time and that neither he nor Keel would say such things in even a jesting manner if they had been in the locale, so he pressed his friend for details.
>
> "Well, damn near everywhere I go the witness has been given a copy of one of the Steiger-Whitenour books or a magazine with an article in it by you or Keel!"

"And the books and articles are supposed to frighten them?" Steiger questioned. "Whoever is delivering these things must be adding their own interpretation...Who are the delivery boys? Have you seen them?"

"Not until this afternoon," the newsman answered. "I guess I arrived at this farmhouse just a few minutes after they did. Damn unfriendly little monkeys...I was trying to talk to the farmer's wife, while they were chattering at the farmer and waving a copy of this magazine in their hands and telling the man how Brad Steiger was warning all UFO sighters not to talk."

"Could you describe them?"

"They were short men in dark suits. All three of them had deep suntans...I can't recall even seeing their eyes. Come to think of it, they all wore dark glasses."

Small wonder there's so much paranoia in the UFO field. These mystery men have posed as Air Force officers, well-known investigators, and members of the amateur UFO organizations, deliberately sowing confusion and fear in their wake. There are even reliable reports describing entities who resembled exactly the men they were imitating *(doppelgängers)*. On several occasions these *doppelgängers* have visited witnesses who had been previously interviewed by the author, creating considerable confusion. The Colorado University study tried to shrug off the Heflin photos because of the "internal inconsistencies" in his story: his visits from nonexistent military officers. Similar episodes have led to extended feuds between amateur investigators and groups, each believing that the other has been warning witnesses not to talk to them.

In many of these episodes, the MIB appear on the scene immediately after the sightings, before the witness has had a chance to report it to anyone. They often flourish an identification card and announce they are from Washington or the CIA (any real CIA agent who went around openly identifying himself as such would soon be standing in an unemployment line). When they use the Air Force ploy, they have the uncanny ability to use the name of an existing officer, but they change their rank. Thus a Colonel Higgins may turn up in a flap area where an actual sergeant named Higgins is stationed nearby.

Adding to the nonsense and confusion, we have the dreary fact that ufology has always attracted eccentric personalities, and a few (very few) of these situations have proven to be their doing. One quasi-scientific UFO group maintains an office in Washington, D.C., and some of their members are fond of waving their membership cards about authoritatively, giving the false impression that they represent a government agency.

The whole mess began in Tacoma in 1947. Since then, the MIB manifestations have created a body of myth and lore fingering the federal government as the sinister silencer of UFO witnesses and censor of UFO news in the press. (There is no UFO censorship, as the publication of this book attests.) The hardcore UFO buffs maintain these myths, however. They ignore the massive evidence found in the other frames of reference that points to the puzzling existence of the parahuman mimics of man who have always been engaged in mischievous—and sometimes malicious—shenanigans.

Mrs. Coral Lorenzen, who ran the Aerial Phenomena Research Organization (APRO) from 1952 until her death in 1988, devoted a chapter of her book, *UFOs over the Americas*, to the CIA's purportedly sinister interest in the subject. Her guidance was a combination of hearsay, speculation, coincidences, classic MIB manipulations, and the uneasy feeling that APRO was being watched. It is not surprising, of course, that some of the UFO organizations have occasionally been monitored by the FBI and other agencies, since the leading proponents of UFO beliefs have made a habit of publicly attacking the government and the military establishment on radio and television. Some UFO publications do border on the subversive. In the 1950s, a strong Communist influence was visible, and some major groups collapsed when they turned more political than ufological. In the 1960s, ufology swung in the other direction, as members of the extreme right wing embraced the flying saucer cause. In 1969 the long-suffering Air Force got out of the UFO business by closing down Project Blue Book, its half-hearted flying saucer agency, thus eliminating the favorite target of the UFO cultists' wrath.

Another group of CIA-baiting researchers is now overlapping into ufology. They are the comparatively small teams of amateur sleuths dedicated to investigating the assassination of President Kennedy. Here the black

Cadillacs and the slight, dark men in black suits are viewed as Cubans and CIA agents. Paranoia runs high because now over fifty witnesses, reporters, and assassination investigators have met with sudden death, some under the most suspicious circumstances. The full story of Kennedy's murder in Dallas in 1963 is filled with incredible details, many of them similar to things found in the most mysterious of the UFO incidents. Photos and physical evidence have vanished or been tampered with just as in so many UFO cases. A wide assortment of mystery men have been involved, including *doppelgängers* of the late Lee Harvey Oswald.* This other Oswald even turned up at a public rifle range before the assassination, making a nuisance of himself (so the witnesses would be sure to remember him?) as he fired an unusual gun which spat out balls of fire at the target. He also visited an automobile showroom and went for a demonstration ride in a new car. The real Oswald could not drive. His whereabouts at the time of these incidents are known...and he was nowhere near the rifle range and auto agency.

The huge *Warren Report* contains numerous pieces of sworn testimony describing MIB-type men in the vicinity of Dealey Plaza and the School Book Depository building immediately before and after the assassination. Long-haired men were seen. This may not sound extraordinary, but remember that long hair was most unusual in 1963. The Beatles did not begin to make an impression until 1964, and the long-hair fad did not get underway until 1965–66.

Elemental hair styles have always been on the longish side, as we have already noted. The UFO lore is filled with accounts of pilots with angular faces and long, shoulder-length hair, usually blond, just as the gods, demons, and angels of earlier times sported long hair. Another interesting consistency is the unnatural color of their hair...so unnatural that witnesses often comment on it. The late Mrs. Mary Hyre, a newspaper reporter in Point Pleasant, West Virginia, received visits from strange personages soon after she began to write about local UFO sightings. Two of these strangers had long,

---

*See Richard Popkin, *The Second Oswald*.

silver hair, she said: "They were young men, and I couldn't understand why they had dyed their hair such a funny color."

Mrs. Hyre also claimed encounters with darkly tanned, soberly dressed gentlemen who rode up to her office in black Cadillacs. One of them asked her what she would do if someone ordered her to stop publishing UFO reports.

"I'd tell them to go to hell," was her reply.

Jerome Clark, one of America's leading ufologists, has his own theory about the present trend toward long hair. "For a long time contactees and their followers talked freely of the New Age, while the rest of us…merely sneered," Clark wrote in *Flying Saucer Review,* September-October 1970. "Now there is considerable talk, even a popular song, about the coming of the Aquarian Age. One of the features of the New Age, as contactees predicted years ago, is the revival of interest in the occult: astrology, the Tarot, palmistry, telepathy, spiritualism, magic, witchcraft, the ouija board, and so on. Also involved, of course, are such obvious features as changes in clothing and hair styles…On basic strategic grounds, it is easier now for 'them' to walk in our midst unnoticed (a long-haired blond male, for example, would now attract little if any attention in the streets of most good-sized Western cities, nor would 'strange' behavior patterns be any particular cause for alarm in a culture born of nonconformity)."

There are millions of people today who do believe that Venusians, Martians, angels, and demons are walking among us unnoticed, their long hair and peculiar dress and manners no longer attracting attention. Strange men in black turtleneck sweaters and wraparound sunglasses (a favorite garb of our MIB) are being reported everywhere. The black Cadillacs are on the prowl.

Have we been invaded by beings from outer space or from some other space-time continuum, as so many now believe, or is it that we are just beginning to notice the funny folk who have been in our midst all along?

In any case it is understandable that so many researchers and investigators double-bolt their doors at night and spend their days peering fearfully over their shoulders.

Chapter Ten

Rendezvous With the Damned

SOMETIME AROUND THE YEAR A.D. 421 a group of artisans from a now lost civilization painstakingly engraved a series of gold leaves or plates with cryptic symbols and buried them in a stone box on the west side of a hill near what is now the village of Manchester, New York. They remained there, unknown and untouched for fourteen hundred years. Then on Friday, September 21, 1821, an eighteen-year-old farm boy named Joseph Smith awoke to a vision in his bedroom near Palmyra, New York. A personage appeared, he said later, "...standing in the air, for his feet did not touch the floor." This being, dressed in a long robe "of most exquisite whiteness," was surrounded by light, and "his countenance was truly like Lightning." He identified himself as Moroni, a "messenger sent from the presence of God," called the youth by name, and announced that he had been chosen for a special task. In subsequent appearances Moroni gave Joseph Smith the exact location of the box and told him that he was to dig it up when instructed to do so.

Six years passed before Smith received word to unearth the tablets. The date was September 22, 1827. That night the skies were aflame with a spectacular display of meteors, falling stars, and luminous spheres. One of the many witnesses was another young man who lived in northern New York but was unacquainted with Joseph Smith. His name was Brigham Young.

Smith dug into the hillside, found the box exactly as Moroni had said, pried off the lid, and discovered the gold plates along with crystalline devices which became known as the *Urim* and *Thummin*. He spent the next three years translating the strange writing—although he had little formal education—purportedly with the aid of the lenslike objects. Eleven of his friends and neighbors signed formal affidavits swearing they had viewed the plates. But once they had been translated, the gold plates vanished. "The messenger called for them," Smith explained.

In March 1830 the translation was published by a local printer. It was the *Book of Mormon*, a history of ancient North America. The following month the Mormon Church was officially organized with six members in Fayette, New York. Today it has over 4.5 million followers.

Joseph Smith was murdered by a hostile mob in Carthage, Illinois, in June 1844. Brigham Young became the leader of the harassed band of Mormons, who worked their way across the country until they arrived at the rather inhospitable wasteland around the Great Salt Lake in Utah. In 1848, many of the Mormons were dismayed by Young's choice for the site of their future city. But a year later the California Gold Rush began and the gold-mad hordes charging westward all paused at Salt Lake City for supplies. Within a short time the city was prospering, and many of the Mormons became rich overnight.

This is essentially the history—and the legend—of the Mormons. The controversy that raged around the authenticity of the *Book of Mormon* and its teachings is too complicated to discuss here. The point is this: there is enough evidence to believe that a specter, a vision, or an angel visited Joseph Smith, or else he ascertained the location of those plates by some psychic ability—or by pure accident. And wouldn't it be interesting if the story were entirely true? If the elementals, ultraterrestrials, or some other force did select Joseph Smith, passed along the information about the plates, and engineered the formation of the Mormon religion?

All of our great religions were founded in almost the same way. Muhammad (A.D. 570–632) was just an Arab tradesman until at the age of forty he began to have visions and conversations with messengers, which led him to organize the Muslim religion and write the *Koran*. More recent religions, such as the Seventh Day Adventists and Jehovah's Witnesses, were established by men who claimed communication with supernatural beings and often issued amazing prophecies that came true. Throughout history common men have had uncommon experiences that have changed them instantly and in many cases even changed the whole fabric of the period in which they lived. A Jewish tentmaker named Saul was once on the road to Damascus to help suppress the rise of Christianity when, according to tradition, a blinding light appeared in the sky, and a voice converted him on the spot. He became St. Paul.

Two groups of forces have always been involved in this cosmic charade. Early man quickly learned to separate them into the good (prohuman) and evil (antihuman) and gave each new god and demon a name. In the interests of clarity, we shall label the good guys the Alpha Group and the bad guys the Omega Group. The Alpha Group gave man a set of ethics and moral principles, while the Omega Group fostered racism, greed, and violence. As time passed, the two groups began imitating each other's tactics, and the task of discriminating between them became impossibly difficult. In his confusion, man soon began to associate everything that happened around him to one of the groups. Natural catastrophes and accidents were automatically blamed on the Omega Group. This led to the development of pure superstition and the awesome, irrational fear of all ultraterrestrials. Things reached a peak in the Middle Ages. Then every new and radical invention was regarded as an invention of the devil, and men such as Galileo, who came up with new scientific discoveries running contrary to the accepted cosmological view, were jailed or burned at the stake.

The Omega Group delighted in spreading false interpretations of the universe and false religious teachings. For every Buddha and Muhammad there were ten thousand Cyrus Teeds.

Who was Cyrus Teed? He believed that the universe was a sphere and that the earth was hollow and that we live on the inside of it. Born in 1839, Teed took up the study of alchemy in Utica, New York, and at the age of thirty he received his first visit from a beautiful female entity who materialized in his laboratory. Following the pattern of such contacts, she first informed him of his past incarnations. He had been mighty kings and great men in past lives, naturally. (No one ever approached by these entities has ever been identified as of lesser station.) Then she proceeded to give him a detailed history of the cosmos, complete with her own special terminology, which, of course, he adopted. He began to write pamphlets and books on this new Cellular Cosmogony, became a powerful public speaker, and gradually built a following for his profitable Koreshan cult (he used the pseudonym Koresh). He settled finally in Fort Myers, Florida, where he established his New Jerusalem with about two hundred followers. He died in 1908 of injuries resulting from an altercation with the local sheriff.

Teed had promised that he would rise again after death. He was buried in a concrete tomb on the island of Estero, and a violent hurricane carried his tomb off in 1921. His body was never recovered. This event gave the Koreshan cult new impetus, and it survived into the 1940s.

Teed-like ideas permeate the thousands of books written in every language by percipients and contactees. He proposed, for example, the existence of a supersun that served as the ultimate source of the universe. Albert K. Bendei claimed that the space people described this central body to him also. Many variations of this concept exist in the literature. Long before Albert Einstein published his famous theory of relativity in 1905, Einsteinian ideas were being expounded by the ultraterrestrials and published by enthused percipients. The Big Bang Theory currently in favor with leading astronomers is that the universe began when all matter was condensed in a single point, which then exploded. The fragments of that explosion, including our own solar system, are now hurling outwards from the center at tremendous velocity, but eventually they will follow the curvature of space as envisioned by Einstein and return to reform a new central body. Then the whole cycle will start over again. Teed and his ilk have been talking about this same thing in their own peculiar way for centuries.

Scientists and doctors who have examined people claiming visions and visits with ultraterrestrials have been puzzled by their apparent normality. In many cases the percipients have seemed too unintelligent, unimaginative, uneducated, and too sincere to have simply invented the complicated, profusely detailed stories they relate. The contactee syndrome is not a form of insanity, but insanity—particularly paranoid schizophrenia—frequently develops after the contacts begin. Investigators, however, are still debating which came first in some cases—insanity or contact.

The first complete psychological study of a percipient took place in the 1890s, when Theodore Flournoy, a professor of psychology at the University of Geneva, investigated the strange phenomena surrounding a girl known as Helene Smith. Beginning in March 1892, Miss Smith started to receive messages through automatic writing (a process in which the percipient merely holds the pen and some other force moves it). Soon she was going into trances and speaking in a man's voice with an Italian accent. He identified himself as Leopold and proved to be something of a rascal, prefacing his communications with phrases such as, "I am here. I wish to be master of this sitting." Then all kinds of poltergeistic activity would begin. Later, however, Victor Hugo, the deceased author, came through the medium and offered advice on how to handle the evil Leopold.

The clash between Leopold and Victor Hugo escalated into a classic ultraterrestrial game, just as the modern UFO contactees are caught up in the games waged between the spacemen and the evil Men in Black. Then at 3:15 A.M., on the morning of September 5, 1896, Helene woke up and had a strange vision. She viewed, she said, a foreign landscape with a "beautiful blue-pink lake" whose shores were joined by a transparent bridge. A crowd of "peculiar people" approached the bridge. A man "of dark complexion, carrying an instrument somewhat resembling a carriage lantern in appearance, which, being pressed, emitted flames and which seemed to be a flying machine" stood on the center of the bridge. Using this instrument, he flew off the bridge, touched the water, and flew back again.

By the end of that September, the dark-complexioned man had become a part of Helene's life. He appeared and disappeared suddenly when she was alone and fully conscious. Often he spoke to her in a strange, unknown tongue. His name was Astane, and he was from Mars, he told her soberly. He looked more like an Oriental or East Indian. On a number of occasions he guided her to his home on Mars, at least in her visions and hallucinations. Usually he was dressed in beautifully embroidered robes. Miss Smith described at length the vehicles on Mars, stating they had neither wheels nor horses, and people seemed to fly about in them.

Helene quickly learned to speak the strange Martian language. Her auto-matic writing also developed a new twist. She began writing in unknown sym-bols and gradually over many months Professor Flournoy was able to decipher them and translate Martian into French. These symbols had the Oriental char-acteristics that have been so often described by modern flying saucer con-tactees who claim to have been aboard the craft. In later periods, Helene would sometimes lapse into this language in the course of normal conversation with-out realizing she was doing so. It was not, Flournoy noted, the kind of gib-berish that children make up when they are playing at being Chinese or Indian. It was an actual language that could be broken down and studied.

Other Martians turned up answering to the names of Ramie and Esenale. Soon Helene's world was peopled with strange beings with long hair and long fingers (both common characteristics of the UFO entities described by contactees) who led her off on spiritual trips to other planets.

On November 2, 1898, Helene reported rising at 6:15 A.M. and feeling an invisible arm clasp itself about her waist. "I then saw myself surrounded by a rose-colored light which generally shows itself when a Martian vision is coming," she said. She found herself suddenly in "a section of country peo-pled by men altogether different from those who inhabit our globe. The tallest of all were three feet high, and the majority were an inch or two shorter. Their hands were immense, about ten inches long by eight inches broad; they were ornamented with very long black nails. Their feet were also of great size."

These little men of 1898 resided in simple houses "all low, long, with-out windows or doors; and each house had a little tunnel about ten feet long running from it into the earth. The roofs were flat, supplied with chimneys or tubes."

All of the things described in Flournoy's 447-page study, *From India to the Planet Mars*, published in 1900, have been repeated endlessly in the occult and UFO literature in other cases. The little men have since earned a special place in flying saucer lore. Flournoy speculated that Leopold and Astane could have been the same entity in different guises. Perhaps he was aware of Swedenborg's warning centuries earlier that the ultraterrestrials could assume any identity, and more interestingly, if the percipient accepted their identity, they would eventually believe themselves that they were Moses, Napoleon, or Astane. Joseph Smith and his friends were treated with visits not only from Moroni but also from entities claiming to be John the Baptist and the apostles Peter, James, and John.

Our ultraterrestrials are ham actors who delight in assuming roles and adopting names from ancient mythology. Early theologians were kept busy recording the endless names of angels and demons. Numbers are also flourished indiscriminately in both religious and contactee literature. The Bible contains long chapters giving elaborate but seemingly meaningless measurements. In *Oahspe,* a book produced by automatic writing in 1880, we learn that Egypt had a population of thirteen million at the time of Moses' birth; four million of these were enslaved Hebrews. (Today Egypt's population is about fifty-five million—not much of an increase in two thousand years.) Page after page in *Oahspe* lists the total number of spirits and angels and druks (the *Oahspe* word for the Omega Group). This numbers game has been extended to the modern UFO phenomena. On August 7, 1965, three prominent men in Venezuela were present at a UFO landing and had a conversation with two tall (seven to eight feet) beings with long yellow hair, large penetrating eyes, and one-piece metallic coverall-type garments. The witnesses, who included a well-known Venezuelan doctor, claimed they communicated through telepathy, and among the questions they asked was, "Are there any beings like you living among us?"

"Yes," came the reply. "Two million, four hundred and seventeen thousand, eight hundred and five."

That's a very precise answer. But many other contactees have thought to ask the same question, and the answers are wildly variable...from seventy-five to ten thousand (in the city of Los Angeles alone) to up in the millions. Our long-haired friends also indulge in nonsensical prophecy on a grand scale. Asked when the world is going end, they are apt to give a precise date in the near future. Some people have actually started building arks on their say-so. One group in Denmark erected a hasty atom bomb shelter in 1967 and settled down to await Armageddon that December. Who is going to be elected president in the next election? The elementals announce with grave authority that Frank Sinatra or Mae West is in line for the job.

The study of glossolalia has had a small group of scholarly followers for years. This is the attempted translation of the mysterious language(s) spoken by the ultraterrestrials, mediums, and church groups who indulge in speaking in tongues. It seems to be a conglomerate of many languages, both ancient and modern, and Flournoy wasn't the first to try to unravel it. There are books filled with symbols and translations similar to, but never exactly like, Helene Smith's Martian language. Dozens of these phony alphabets have been published in dead seriousness. A retired schoolteacher named John W. Dean collected the testimony of flying saucer contactees and the elaborate information passed along by the space people for his book, *Flying Saucers Close Up*. The project must have taken years. He devotes many pages to listing unknown planets far out in the cosmos (as described by the ultraterrestrials), and giving encyclopedic data about each one.

Here's a sample from one of his tables:

Planet Name	Colonized, Indigenous, Uninhabited	Population in Billions	Day Length in Hours	Diameter in Miles	Year Length
Warnovaldam	Un.	—	36.6	7,188	0.95
Tarmandre	Col.	1.20	23.7	9,170	1.88
Ophianche	Ind.	3.62	28.0	10,480	3.21
Salumandran	Ind.	4.23	24.1	9,810	5.66

Dean lists hundreds of unknown planets in this fashion. The group in this particular table happens to be from the star system of Alpha Tauri, 53.6 light years away. But anyone with a basic knowledge of orbital mechanics and a slide rule can check the mass of figures and discover that many of these alleged planetary systems are quite impossible. The cosmos of the ultraterrestrials must be filled with colliding planets weaving and spinning in defiance of all the known laws of motion.

In *Flying Saucers Close Up,* Mr. Dean also presents a complete vocabulary and the written language of the folks from the planet called Korendor. Some of the symbols bear a striking resemblance to runic ciphers. His book is only a minor example of the privately published material circulated to about two thousand hardcore flying saucer believers. Over the past twenty years the ultraterrestrials have constructed a whole fantasy world through the contactees—a cosmos that includes great Intergalactic Councils (as soon as we grow up, we may be permitted to join).

On other levels, in different frames of reference believers speak in terms of other planes. The most common belief shared by every culture on this planet is that there are seven distinct worlds or realities. We live on the lowest rung of the ladder. If there is a hell, we must be living in it.

Numerous religious sects are concerned with Holy Ghost apparitions and the speaking in tongues phenomenon, which they accept as verification of their beliefs. The United Pentecostal Church, for example, finds great meaning in such manifestations...and they occur constantly within the church. Church bulletins and publications are filled with accounts of these events. The newsletter, *Global Witness*, June-July 1970, described the following, as reported by a group in Peru:

> On April 28th as they were praying, the ten-year-old daughter suddenly went into what they thought was a "fit of convulsions." She began to jerk and shake all over. Her terrified mother rushed to her side to attempt to help her daughter, but an unseen hand restrained her, and a voice urged her to leave the girl alone. In just a few moments this little girl, who did not know what the Holy Ghost was, began to speak in a strange but lovely new language. The following Tuesday night the oldest boy was marvelously filled with the Holy Ghost. He rejoiced in the Spirit and spoke with tongues for over an hour.

Convulsive seizures are common to all the frames of reference. Many UFO contactees suffer chronic headaches, muscular soreness, and other symptoms of such seizures after their experiences. These fits could be caused by some disorder of the frontal lobe of the brain or by some electromagnetic wave directed at the frontal lobe. Primitive peoples usually regarded such fits as demonic possessions.

One of the world's foremost psychologists, Dr. Carl G. Jung, examined the socio-religious aspects of the UFO rumors and published a shrewd analysis, *Flying Saucers: A Modern Myth of Things Seen in the Sky* in 1959. He correlated the UFO reports with psychic manifestations and suggested that the phenomena were products of the collective consciousness of mankind. "The psychic aspect plays so great a role that it cannot be left out of account," Dr. Jung stated. "The discussion of it leads to psychological problems which involve just as fantastic possibilities or impossibilities as the approach from the physical side."

Another scientist, Dr. Jacques Vallee, an astronomer and computer specialist, spent several years sifting UFO accounts and comparing them with the earlier fairy lore of Europe. He felt that the two phenomena shared a single cause. In *Passport to Magonia* (1969), Vallee offered a catalog of 923 flying saucer landings from 1868 to 1968, many of which included the classic characteristics of the more universal psychic manifestations. "Is it reasonable to draw a parallel between religious apparitions, the fairy faith, the reports of dwarflike beings with supernatural powers, the airship tales in the United States in the last century, and the present stories of UFO landings?" he asks. "I would strongly argue that it is—for one simple reason: *the mechanisms that have generated these various beliefs are identical.*"

The crux of the problem is to reach beyond the endless reports of varied manifestations and seek out the source: the physical, psychic, or psychological mechanism which has inspired these beliefs. All of these incidents are subjective; that is, we have only the testimony of the witnesses that these peculiar events occurred. Although millions of people have claimed encounters with the ultraterrestrials in the past two thousand years, many millions of others have not had such experiences. Astronomers and physicists are neither trained nor equipped to deal with a purely subjective phenomenon.

Only a few examples have been given, but it is apparent that Joseph Smith, Cyrus Teed, Helene Smith, and even John Dean were all confronted by the same basic phenomenon. Each approached it in a different, individualized way, and each received information structured to support his own beliefs. Albert K. Bender and Teed both explored black magic and alchemy. Both claimed they received complex cosmic theories from parahuman entities. Dean asked for and received elaborate facts and figures about extraterrestrial beings and the planets they supposedly inhabited. Like Swedenborg and the biblical prophet Enoch, Helene Smith was shown other worlds and led to believe that she was visiting other planets. Reinhold Schmidt was transported to the center of the pyramid; Bender was taken to underground bases in Antarctica; others have visited the underground palaces of the fairies and the subterranean cities of the Deros. It is not likely that any of these places exist in reality. It is more likely that these people made hallucinogenic excursions, or mind trips, guided by some force which is capable of manipulating the electrical circuits of the brain.

The only alternative explanation is that all these people were liars and hoaxsters or lunatics. None of the scientists, psychiatrists, and theologians who have investigated these matters have been able to accept such a simple explanation.

A remarkable man named Aleister Crowley, born in 1875, became known as the wickedest man in the world through his work in black "magick." He too claimed to receive visits from an angel, and he was the center of a large cult around the turn of the century. He was noted for sexually liberating his female followers, and he published a number of books expounding on his personal cosmology. Those books enjoyed a revival of popularity among the youth subculture in the sixties and seventies, and more of them are now in print than ever before.

In 1939, a young rocket fuel scientist, John Whiteside Parsons, joined the Crowley cult and burrowed into the dark world of "magick" and the occult. Another practitioner of the mysteries crossed Parsons' path in 1946, and the two became close friends, combining their efforts to conjure up demons and elementals. The newcomer claimed he had a personal angel, a beautiful red-haired entity whom he called the Empress. The two men donned robes and engaged in secret mystical rites. According to Parsons, they had some success. On the night of January 14, 1946, the electric power failed as they were mumbling incantations, and his companion was struck by something on the right shoulder, knocking a candle from his hand. "He called me," Parsons wrote, "and we observed a brownish-yellow light about seven-feet high. I brandished a magical sword, and it disappeared. His right arm was paralyzed for the rest of the night."

His fellow practitioner demonstrated his friendship by stealing Parsons' girlfriend, Betty. Then he proposed a business venture and got Parsons to put up seventeen thousand dollars. The next thing Parsons knew, the fellow had purchased a yacht and sailed off to Florida with Betty. In a letter to the aging Crowley dated July 5, 1946, Parsons said, "Here I am in Miami, pursuing the children of my folly. I have them well tied up. They can not move without going to jail. However, I am afraid that most of the money has already been spent. I will be lucky to salvage three to five thousand dollars.... [The "friend"] attempted to escape me by sailing at 5 P.M. and performed the full invocation to Bartzabel [a curse]. At the same time, however, his ship was struck by a sudden squall off the coast, which ripped off his sails and forced him back to port, where I took the boat in custody."

During one of their rites, Parsons was given this prophecy: "Babalon [the whore of Babylon] is incarnate upon the earth today, awaiting the proper hour of her manifestation. And in that day my work will be accomplished, and I shall be blown away upon the breath of the father...."

A rocket fuel explosion at a laboratory in Pasadena in 1952 did blow away the ill-fated Parsons.

The games of the ultraterrestrials never end.

Another entry in the great celestial con is an outfit called Koscot Interplanetary, Inc., of Orlando, Florida, who have "had difficulties with law enforcement agencies in several states," according to the Better Business Bureau. Koscot has been pushing "Dare To Be Great," a motivational course consisting of a series of four tapes that will tell you how to get rich. The four tapes cost only seventy-seven hundred dollars, but the investment can be quickly recouped by selling the course to others. The whole scheme is based upon a pyramid plan with each student peddling the course to new seekers of truth. Unfortunately, the population of a state cannot support an indefinite selling plan that depends on recruiting other sellers and students, and the Better Business Bureau has labeled the whole enterprise "doubtful and unrealistic." The tapes deal largely with the same philosophy and cosmology found in all the occult lore.

Chapter Eleven

Not One of Them

Not One of Them Who Took Up in His Youth With This Opin-
ion That There Are No Gods Ever Continued Until Old Age
Faithful to His Conviction.   —Plato

A NEW JERSEY SIGN PAINTER named Howard Menger experienced a most
revealing flying saucer vision in August, 1956, when he came face-to-face
with a godlike being. But according to his book, *From Outer Space to You*,
Menger's story began years earlier. As a boy he had encountered a beautiful
female entity in a woods and was told that he would one day serve the illustrious space people. As a young man in the Army he was contacted again,
this time in Juarez, Mexico, by a man with long blond hair and sun-tanned
skin, riding in a taxicab. Then in the mid-1950s, Menger's real adventures
began. Strange aerial objects haunted the area around his home near High
Bridge, New Jersey. (There were innumerable witnesses, including lawyers,
physicists, and reporters.) The space people began to drop in on him for cof-
fee and friendly chats about the state of the universe. They asked him to buy
dark sunglasses with red lenses, and on several occasions they even pressed
him into service as a barber, inviting him to chop off their long blond tresses
so they would look even more human. He was rewarded with a flight to the
moon (he brought back some strange rocks which were, he said, moon pota-
toes). Finally, in August 1956, he met the boss spaceman.

A saucer landed in a field near Menger's home, and two men stepped
out of it. "Then a magnificent sight appeared in the doorway," Menger wrote.
"A tall, handsome man with long blond hair over his shoulders stood towering

115

at the entrance...Then he came toward me. But he seemed to float or glide rather than walk." This being was dressed in "a radiant white ski-type uniform...the sleeves were full and loose; the neckline was high, similar to that of a turtleneck sweater." He wore a light blue, fluorescent-like cape fastened to his shoulder with a gold pin in the shape of a wheel. His skin was white, and his eyes "were the color of goldenrod when it is ripe." His fingers were long and tapering.

This superbeing gave Menger a message of love and truth in the grand tradition of the elementals, then returned to his flying saucer and flew off to the stars.

When Howard Menger courageously published his story (it was privately printed in 1959), he was roundly cheered by one group of cultists for having solved the UFO mystery and roundly condemned by the equally fanatical scientific ufologists who believed in the existence of extraterrestrial spaceships but could not believe that anyone had ever been close to one. His business collapsed as he gained a reputation for being a crackpot, and his family fell apart.

If Howard Menger had lived in another age, he might have been looked upon as a great prophet and visionary—one of those privileged individuals who consorted with the gods. Sculptors would have been commissioned to carve mighty replicas of the superbeing. Poems and songs would have been written about his experience and handed down from one generation to the next.

Unfortunately, Menger lived in 1956. He was laughed out of business. His book earned a few hundred dollars from sales to the hardcore cultists and was then forgotten. But it is a revealing record of the mechanism of belief which is at work in these cases. If such things could happen in 1956, then they may also have happened in 1056 and 556 B.C. There are in fact extensive legends suggesting that this sort of thing has been happening to men since the beginning of history. The long-haired, long-fingered ultraterrestrials have been walking among us forever.

Before we can understand this tangled maze, we must attempt to understand something of the origins and complexities of human history. We must try to ascertain how it all began, how the ultraterrestrials have influenced our course, and where it is all leading us.

Our scientists can only guess at how the universe itself came into being. The two most popular theories are the Big Bang concept, already discussed, and the Steady State theory that matter is constantly replenishing itself and that the cosmos really has no beginning or end. The beginning of the solar system and the birth of the planets are a little easier to deal with. The commonly accepted theory is that the planets are cooling masses of material ejaculated from the sun.

Two independent scientists, Dr. C. J. Hyman and C. William Kinsman, developed a geocosmic theory based upon the discoveries outlined in earlier chapters, coupled with Velikovsky-like evidence and speculations. They suggested that earth once pursued the orbit now occupied by Venus and that Mars was in the present earth orbit. This would explain the legends of early man, which claimed that earth days and years were once shorter than they are now and that the human life span was once considerably longer. Ancient calendars carved in stone also indicate important differences in the early earth year. If the earth began as a lump of matter cast off by the sun, it may have first passed along the orbit of Mercury before spiraling outward and settling into the orbit of Venus. This could have happened five billion years ago.

The cooling planet earth could have reached the life-support stage hundreds of millions of years ago, and it could have been inhabited while it was in the Venus orbit. If Mars was then in the earth orbit, it too could have supported life. But as it was pushed further into space by the approach of earth, the Martians either died out or were forced to make radical biological adjustments to their new environment.

In a letter, Kinsman also proposed that there was some effort to crossbreed Martians with earthlings. He stated:

If Mars was "pushed" out there in our Permian times to make way for earth in our present orbits, its environmental change in climate in this some three hundred million years would surely modify its humanoids, because of the scarcity of air, water, and warmth, into presumably a more scrawny physique no longer adapted to normal life on earth... Presumably for millions of years they have been trying to hybridize their fauna and flora with ours and to develop some sort of humanoid to whom they could bequeath the advances which their dying civilization had long since acquired. Success in this seems to have finally come with the sudden hybrid appearance of Cro-Magnon man some fifty thousand years ago. They may have visited us frequently and openly for such time as they could stand it, until a few millennia ago (when men were still few and fearful).

If the earth did begin in another orbit and did undergo the changes postulated by these scientists, it may have been even more unstable than it is now and cataclysmic occurrences would have been logical. Velikovsky pointed out that human folklore has recorded many such cataclysms, including a period when the entire earth was bathed in total darkness for three or more days. The earth may have followed an elliptical orbit which carried it so far away from the sun that it was plunged into darkness. Then it looped back and fell into the present orbit.

Elementals have constantly told occultists and UFO contactees that mankind began on Venus and that orbital changes have taken place in the past and will recur in the future. On April 24, 1964, a farmer named Gary Wilcox allegedly had a two-hour conversation with a pair of faceless little men from a flying saucer in a field near Newark Valley, New York. Among other things, he said, they told him that the earth would soon be where Mars is now.*

Many flying saucer books have followed the premise that the earth was originally seeded by beings from outer space. Man has always assumed that the frequently observed parahumans *had* to originate from beyond our planet or even from beyond our solar system or space-time continuum.

Science writer Otto Binder's *Flying Saucers Are Watching Us* dealt at length with the theories of an engineer named Max H. Flindt. Flindt proposed that man is a hybrid from the union of ancient spacemen and some earthly species of man-ape who existed, according to recent anthropologic finds, as long as five million years ago.

---

*Dr. Berthold Schwarz's psychiatric study of Mr. Wilcox in *UFO Percipients*.

More orthodox scientists have struggled for the past hundred years to find a provable system of evolution to account for man's appearance. The commonly accepted view is that man was a mere animal for thousands of years, and he somehow suddenly developed intelligence and consciousness and quickly evolved from a low hairy animal to his present exalted status of low hairless animal. The mythical missing link of the Sunday supplements is supposed to be the animal that bridged the two orders of life. In the movie, *2001*, Arthur C. Clarke solved the problem by having a sudden outside influence— the slab-like monolith—appear in the midst of a group of apes. It led them to discover tools, namely clubs, and they began bashing in each other's heads.

There are really only three primary theories for the origin of man:

1. The religious theory: man was created by some greater intelligence through the manipulation of physical matter and energy.
2. The cultist theory: man migrated to earth from some other planet, or he was seeded here by some other race, or he was produced when some other race crossbred with earthly animals and produced the present strain of *Homo sapiens.*
3. The theory of evolution: a series of random chemical and biological accidents took place over a period of millions of years, and man slowly evolved from lower life forms.

Billions of people have believed and still believe in supernatural creation. A few million accept Darwin's theory of evolution, and only a few thousand are even willing to consider the seeded idea. The real truth may be a combination of all three. Of the three, evolution is actually the weakest and the most difficult to support. Evolution adequately explains the development of living species, the process of natural selection, and other things, but it fails to provide a rational and provable explanation for the process of creation itself. Scientists shrug this off with limp statements about how bolts of lightning struck puddles of chemicals and induced life. But if such a lightning process were true, it should be still continuing, and it should be easy to duplicate in our laboratories. The fact that it is not a discernible continuing process (new species are not constantly appearing) and that we have not managed to duplicate it weakens the concept.*

The Japanese have myths and legends which claim that their islands were first settled by beings who descended from the sky. These stories are a part of the Japanese culture. The Eskimos believe they were somehow flown to the Arctic circle in ancient times. The natives of the Sahara desert have folklore about blue-skinned people from the sky who had such impact that certain tribes still dye their skins blue in emulation of these ancient cosmic beings. Deep in the Bayan-Kara-Ula Mountains of China there is a tribe of diminutive people about four feet high. Hieroglyphs have been found in that region (on the border of China and Tibet) by Russian archaeologists. When translated, these records describe how members of the Dropa tribe came to earth in some kind of flying machine. The stone disks bearing these inscriptions have been dated at about twelve thousand years. Ancient graves have also been found there containing small human bodies with huge craniums and underdeveloped skeletons.

There is, in fact, a staggering amount of historical and archaeological evidence to support the seeded notion, while the evolutionists are obliged to fall back on a few fragments of fossils and a mountain of conjecture.

The concept of supernatural creation is wholly dependent upon the religious texts and the testimony of the ultraterrestrials. The story of Adam and Eve can be found in the ancient writings of the Greeks, Syrians, Egyptians, Abyssinians, Hebrews, and many other ancient peoples. Like the tales of the deluge and the Ark, the Garden of Eden is a universal myth. Unlike the deluge stories, it seems to be largely allegorical. Archaeologists digging in the Middle East have found artifacts which indicate that Neanderthal, Cro-Magnon, and modern men all existed during the same period. This not only shoots down the theory of evolution, but it suggests that modern man—a

---

*Much has made of the Miller-Urey experiment in the early fifties when conditions that supposedly existed on earth million of years ago were simulated in a closed container and subjected to high-energy sparks ("lightning"). They succeeded in producing amino acids. However, there is as much difference between amino acids and the simplest possible one-celled organism as there is between a hunk of iron ore and a BMW.—ED.

creature with a conscience and a consciousness—was separate and distinct from primitive man.

If we ever manage to assemble a more accurate history of earth, we may find that modern man is the descendant of the survivors of some earlier civilization that existed thousands, even millions, of years ago, and that he has no direct biological linkage with the lower animals at all. We must not ignore the possibility that the earth was originally *colonized* by beings from some other point in space. Historians and archaeologists are troubled by the fact that mankind seems to have *appeared* quite suddenly on this planet. Either we were placed here, even stranded here, at some point between thirty and seventy thousand years ago, or we were created in some fashion millions of years after the earth itself had been created and had passed through many ages during which it supported different kinds of nonhuman life.

The process of creation is explained somewhat in the religious and occult texts. We are told that the first man, Adam, was an androgynous being directly linked with the supermind of the universe. He was a temporary transmogrification of energy—an ultraterrestrial who became locked into a physical form. Once this descent occurred, he was given a mate so that he could reproduce.

The earth was already inhabited by two distinct life forms. There were primitive animals, which might have included cave men as well as lower beasts. Perhaps the cave men were an earlier experiment that was failing. There were also thousands, if not millions, of nonphysical beings from the world of higher frequencies, who occupied the earth by sharing the same space with the planet. These beings may have been free from the greater intelligence (fallen angels), or they may have been under the control of a lesser intelligence. In any case, the earth was their personal playground. *They owned it.*

Now suddenly, a group (or several groups) of ultraterrestrials from a higher plane descended to earth. They were forbidden to do certain things. We can't even guess what those things were. In the scriptures Adam and Eve were forbidden to eat the fruit of the Tree of the Knowledge of Good and Evil. This was probably more symbolism, and the true meaning is lost.

A British scholar, Brinsley Le Peer Trench, has studied the ancient scriptures carefully and produced two important books, *The Sky People* and *Men Among Mankind*, to explain his theories. He describes and defines the people of the Serpent. These people may have been the fallen angels or devils who later plagued Adam and Eve. If they felt they were owners of the earth, they may have greatly resented this new flock of ultraterrestrials, and they may have conspired to lead the Adam and Eve group to destruction by getting them to violate the orders of their overlord.

A battle now takes shape. A lesser group of ultraterrestrials (UTs) is in possession of the earth. A bunch of newcomers invades the planet, and perhaps their ruling intelligence has a plan—a very long-range plan—to wrest the earth from the owners. Masses of energy cannot fight with bombs, bullets, and arrows. They need a physical battlefield and physical armies. The whole thing must be played out like some gigantic chess game.

The first step is to create the necessary physical army. Tactics must be invented so that the physical army can overthrow the nonphysical owners. The game becomes incredibly complex.

If several different superintelligences were involved, then one group of ultraterrestrials would descend or be materialized in Japan and China, bearing the specific racial characteristics imposed upon them by their overlord. Another overlord would plant his soldiers in Africa; another would create Indians in North and South America; and so on.

In the beginning one superintelligence may have tried to utilize the Neanderthal men as his physical army. Ultraterrestrials were sent down the frequency scale to help guide the cave men. To facilitate communication between the UTs and the Neanderthal men, the tall, blond, normally sexless UTs were made to more closely resemble their primitive contacts. They were given sexes but were forbidden to participate in the pleasurable rites of sex...the Tree of the Knowledge.

The Serpent People were sometimes able to control groups of cave men and managed to trick some of the UTs into breaking their chastity. The UTs engaged in sexual intercourse with the cave women.* This produced strange responses in their materialized nervous system. Emotions were born. Frequencies were changed. The direct control of the superintelligence was driven from their bodies. They were trapped on earth, unable to ascend the electromagnetic scale and reenter their etheric world. With the loss of control they became animals, albeit highly intelligent animals.

Since the UT's memories were part of the greater intelligence, the loss of contact meant also the complete loss of their former identity. They were locked on this planet, leaderless, in a totally strange and hostile environment.

The first UTs to be thus trapped became the first real men. They had to learn to hunt and kill, to build fires and huts. They were lost: the victims of the first battle between the Serpent People and the ultimate intelligence.

Now the Serpent People or Omega Group attacked man in various ways, trying to rid the planet of him. But the superintelligence was still able to look over man, and new, more tightly controlled UTs were sent to offer advice and assistance. Earliest man was told in carefully simplified ways of his origin and purpose. The superintelligence became God and early man worshiped Him...in many ways and under many names. God worked out new ways of communication and control, always in conflict with the Serpent People.

Much is made of the fact that Adam and Eve were terrified by the first night, indicating that they were unused to a world without light. Perhaps as ultraterrestrials they were accustomed to total vision or perception of all the frequencies; life on those higher planes would be bathed in continuous radiation, and there would be no night or day. No time. Now Adam and Eve were not only trapped on this miserable little planet, but they were also caught up in a world that moved in a single direction through the field of time. This

---

*This crossbreeding between Adam (ultraterrestrial) types and lower animals is suggested in Genesis 25:19–34, which relates a miraculous birth. Isaac's barren wife Rebekah suddenly conceived, and the Lord said to her, "Two nations are in thy womb, and two manner of people shall be separated from thy bowels; and the one people shall be stronger than the other people; and the elder shall serve the younger." Rebekah gave birth to twins and one, Esau, "came out red all over like an hairy garment." Later Esau sold his birthright to Jacob.

would take some getting used to, even if they couldn't remember their previous existence as UTs.

Through intercourse with the existing cave people, the fallen UTs produced the new races of man. They were the missing link. And in many ways all three of our hypotheses for the origin of man become correct. Evolution is involved. Extraterrestrial descent is involved. Creation is involved.

In some parts of the world the Serpent People successfully posed as gods and imitated the techniques of the superintelligence. This led to the formation of pagan religions centered around human sacrifices. The conflict, so far as man himself was concerned, became one of religions and races. Whole civilizations based upon the worship of these false gods rose and fell in Asia, Africa, and South America. The battleground had been chosen, and the model of conflict had been decided upon.

The human race would supply the pawns. The mode of control was complicated as usual. Human beings were largely free of direct control. Each individual *had to consciously commit himself to one of the opposing forces.* After that commitment was made voluntarily, the chosen force could possess the individual to some degree. The UTs very carefully explained this process to the early priests, who interpreted it and tried to pass it on to their followers. The rites of baptism were born.

The main battle was for what was to become known as the human soul.

Once an individual had committed himself, he opened a door so that an indefinable something (probably an undetectable mass of intelligent energy) could actually enter his body and exercise some control over his subconscious mind. This soul was *directly linked* with the superintelligence and with all similar souls, thus making possible mental telepathy, prophetic dreams, and other wonders. In those thousands of cases in which this subconscious force lapsed over into the conscious mind, we find destructive fanaticism and obsession. If the controlling intelligence is Omega (antihuman), the stricken individual suffers from insanity or commits criminal actions, social disorders, and so on.

If this soul abandons the living body, total disorientation could conceivably result. The body might enter a mindless, catatonic trance. Persons with an advanced soul could consciously eject it from their bodies for short periods and indulge in astral projection. The body would appear to be dead, or almost dead, during this period of desertion. In astral projection literature we are told about a silver cord that seems to connect the free-flying soul with the sleeping body. If that cord is cut or broken, the soul can't reenter the body, and it dies or is possessed by an evil force. Astral projectionists claim that sometimes when they return to their body, they find a dark elemental engulfing it, trying to possess it during their absence, and they have to fight the evil thing off.

The validity of astral projection is debatable, of course. But let's suppose for a moment that it is a genuine phenomenon. If some people can project themselves consciously and remember the experience, then it is also possible that many others project their souls while asleep. They're never aware that they're doing it. The liberated souls fly about, perhaps rendezvousing with other souls to receive orders or some programming process. If the soul is some kind of ultrahigh-frequency energy, then it could be visible to some sensitive people as a blob of faint light in the night sky. In other words, some UFOs could be astral travelers!

Flying saucer contactees usually end up talking about souls and reincarnation (karma). The UFO entities try to convey the truth about reincarnation to the people they approach. Not many of these people are able to properly interpret what they have been told. Several major religions, particularly in the Orient, are based upon the principles of reincarnation. In Tibet before the Chinese takeover, when a Dalai Lama died, the priests went out and scoured the mountains searching for a small child who possessed specific birthmarks and other things that would identify him as the reincarnated High Lama. Sometimes the search went on for years. When a likely prospect was finally found, several religious and personal articles were spread before him. If the child went unerringly for those items that had been owned by the dead Dalai Lama, he was declared the new ruler. This system worked and was in use for centuries.

There are hundreds of carefully investigated and authenticated cases of reincarnation. As might be expected, a majority of these occur in India and other countries where belief in karma runs high. Usually, small children are involved. Such children recall completely their previous life in a distant village, and when investigators take them to that village, they recognize everything and everyone, have a tearful reunion with their former family, and are even able to describe in detail how they died.

Actually, true reincarnation is impossible. Memory is stored by an electrical system in the brain, and when the brain dies, all memories are also canceled out. Our personalities, egos, emotional structure, and memories are all part of the brain's complex circuitry. The brain dies very quickly—as soon as the oxygen supply is cut off. All of this circuitry dies with it, like a radio being turned off. If the soul is merely a mass of high frequency energy, then it would not retain either memory or personality. When the body or host dies, this mass of energy would be liberated either to rejoin the main intelligence of which it is always a part or to find and possess a new host. It would not carry along any memory of its previous body or life. However, the computerlike superintelligence would have a complete memory of that other life stored within it. It could feed that information to another brain by channeling it through any soul at random. A person recalling a past life under hypnosis (there are thousands of cases of this) might actually just be tuning his subconscious into the central computer. There may be some subtle need on the intelligence's part to bring about interest and investigation into a specific past life. So the hypnotized person is fed the information.

In *Oahspe* we are told that all cases of reincarnation are the work of mischievous spirits known as engrafters. An engrafter swoops down on an uncommitted soul and possesses it, feeding a complete memory of a past life into the brain.

The main information passed along to contactees is simply that the human body provides a host for a fragment of this undefinable soul energy. The major religions have been telling us this for thousands of years, pointing out that the human race supplies the shells for souls. Man's ego has demanded that he embellish this truth by adding the belief that his pitiful personality is worthy of preservation and that his memories and personality go along with the soul. The Omega Group has made a game of this belief at millions of seances, happily posing as myriad souls of the dear departed.

Two or more intelligences are playing a game with us, vying for complete control of our bodies and souls, according to all occult and religious interpretations. It's a seesaw battle, and every possible kind of deception and deceit is being employed by both sides. They can make us believe anything they want us to believe, thanks to our swollen egos and flimsy brains. They can make us see anything they want us to see, thanks to our narrow field of vision (we can only see a fragment of the electromagnetic spectrum) and their apparent ability to manipulate energy and physical matter.

The parahuman Serpent People of the past are still among us. They were probably worshiped by the builders of Stonehenge and the forgotten ridge-making cultures of South America. They directed us to multiply and seed the earth. Their manifestations and manipulations have generated thousands of cults, religions, and frames of reference.

In recent years hundreds of UFO contactees have been warned by the long-haired Venusians that our atomic experiments will lead to disaster. Could it be, as some have said, that atomic bombs not only kill cities, but that they also kill or disintegrate souls? If the soul is a fragment of energy linked to some greater mass of intelligent energy, then this anti-atomic-bomb posture of the ultraterrestrials could be defensive. The bomb at Hiroshima may have blown a hole in some other world beyond our space-time continuum...and a lot of moon food may have been lost in the bargain.

Chapter Twelve

The Demise of the Gods

"IF FLYING SAUCERS ARE REAL," the skeptics say, "why don't they contact us?

The startling truth, as carefully recorded by the ancient historians, is that the ultraterrestrials have *always* been in direct contact with millions of individuals and that *they actually ruled directly over mankind for many years.* In recent centuries their influence has become more subtle, but it is always there.

According to the traditions of many isolated peoples, the first great emperors in Asia were god-kings who came down from the sky, displayed amazing superhuman abilities, and took over. There was a veritable worldwide epidemic of these god-kings between 5000 and 1000 B.C. The mighty Osiris and Isis walked into the Egyptian valley out of nowhere and assumed command. The myths and legends of Greece, India, and South America describe their rule. They were taller and more imposing than the men of the time, with long, blond hair, marblelike white skin, and remarkable powers that enabled them to perform miracles. They displayed brilliant judgment and wisdom and exercised remarkable organizational abilities. In most cases they chose to reside on the highest mountains and hills available, commanding balls of fire and bolts of lightning and traveling about the skies in wonderful chariots.

In southern Europe Zeus and his court of phantom cohorts held forth for centuries. In India a multitude of gods and demons appeared and reappeared generation after generation. Others arrived on the scene and made lasting contributions to folklore from Iceland to Scandinavia. In Central America the legendary Quetzalcoatl appeared among the Toltecs. He was a white man dressed in a long white robe covered with tiny red crosses. He wore a great beard and according to Toltec tradition introduced science and learning to the natives. After many years of benign rule he simply vanished, promising to return again one day. When Cortes, the Spanish conquistador, landed in Mexico a thousand years later, the Indians greeted him with delight, believing that he was Quetzalcoatl. He took advantage of their superstition and sacked the Aztec empire.

Deep in the wasteland of western Australia the Aborigines still cling to the ancient myths of the *Wondjina* and regard as sacred the petroglyphs carved into rocks depicting tall, robed figures. The *Wondjina* are supposedly a parahuman group who resided in Australia thousands of years ago.

Berosus, an ancient Babylonian priest, recorded the fascinating legend of Oannes, a remarkable creature who came up out of the waters of the Persian Gulf to educate early man. This legend "more nearly fulfills some of our criteria for a genuine contact myth," Dr. Carl Sagan stated in his *Intelligent Life in the Universe*. Berosus presumably "had access to cuneiform and pictographic records dating back several thousand years before his time." His work was translated into Greek and Latin and found its way into English in 1876. He quoted from Apollodorus, describing Oannes as a fishlike animal capable of speaking to men. The account explains:

> This being in the daytime used to converse with men but took no food at that season; and he gave them an insight into letters and sciences and every kind of art. He taught them to construct houses, to found temples, to compile laws, and explained to them the principles of geometrical knowledge. He made them distinguish the seeds of the earth and showed them how to collect fruits...When the sun set, it was the custom of this being to plunge again into the sea and abide all night in the deep; for he was amphibious.

Moses, of course, had another kind of encounter when he climbed to the summit of Mount Sinai and received orders and laws from the entity who settled there in a glowing cloud.

A central legend of the Hopi Indians concerns the Kachina Clan: a group of beings who were not people but "spirits sent to give help and guidance, taking the forms of ordinary people," according to Indian historian Frank Waters. The Hopi believe they came originally from a Red City in the south and that their tribe was guided into what is now the southwestern United States by the Kachina Clan. These spirit beings taught the Hopis occult wisdom very similar to the occult beliefs of the Europeans and Africans. Finally they departed, saying,

> The time for us to go to our far-off planets and stars has not come yet. But it is time for us to leave you. We will go by our powers to a certain high mountain, which you will know, where we will await your messages of need. We are a spirit people, and we will not be seen again by you or your people. But you must remember us by wearing our masks and our costumes at the proper ceremonial times. Those who do so must be only those persons who have acquired the knowledge and the wisdom we have taught you...

The indigenous natives of the Americas, Africa, and the Pacific all adopted ceremonial dress patterned after the garb of the ultraterrestrials, just as the robes and trappings of the early churches of the white man were patterned after the dress of the angels and gods who allegedly visited them. Traditionally, only the witch doctors and students of the arcane wisdom of the elementals were permitted to wear these garments and masks. The carefully laid-out procedures for the ceremonies and rites of these early peoples were all dictated by these parahuman spirits. For thousands of years they quite literally had the entire human race dancing to their tunes. The impact of these beings upon the human race is indisputable. *All* human art began as part of our urge to pay tribute to them. The arts of painting and sculpture, the arts of drama and dance, and of course, the art of storytelling, were all products of that urge.

It has been impossible to adequately summarize even a fragment of this kind of material here. Perhaps someday some scholar will systematically assemble all of these records and establish some order out of the chaos. The evidence is not as flimsy as this kind of summary might make it seem.

Statues of strange, Oriental-looking figures bearing a striking similarity to the appearance of our contemporary Men in Black have been found in the ruins of the Olmec civilization in Mexico. We really don't know very much about the Olmecs. The first traces of their lost culture were uncovered in 1939, when archaeologist Matthew Stirling found five gigantic basalt heads on the island of La Venta. These heads weigh from twenty to thirty tons each and are up to nine feet high. Each is wearing what looks like a football helmet. Since then, cities and irrigation systems dating back to at least 1200 B.C. have been discovered. An Olmec calendar carved into the stomach of an eight-inch jade statue begins with the year 3113 B.C. "It is a masterpiece of mathematical and astronomical knowledge, and it was the Olmecs, not the Maya, who developed it," Jeanne Reinert noted in *Science Digest* in September 1967.

Archaeologists have come up with an interesting theory for the sexless Oriental-like statues. They suggest that the Olmecs worshiped deformed children and that the statues represent Mongolian idiots. But would a people capable of creating a masterpiece of a calendar worship abnormal babies? The statues also feature a distinctive cleft in their foreheads, and this falls in line with the third eye lore of European occultism, Tibetan beliefs, and even the mysticism of the Hopi Indians. The third eye is supposedly the part of the brain which is linked to ESP and cosmic consciousness—or direct communication with God.

The third eye symbol, an eye inside a triangle, is an ancient symbol for the deity found in many cultures from Egypt to Micronesia. It appears on the Great Seal of the United States atop the pyramid (found on every dollar bill). The Kachina Clan taught the Hopis that an opening in the head existed so they could talk with God. At one time trephination (cutting a hole in the skull) was a common practice throughout the world, perhaps as part of some religious rite. Hundreds of trephinated skulls have been found in Europe, Asia, Africa, the Americas, and the Pacific islands. Many of them date back to 3000 B.C. Some show signs of healing, indicating that the patient must have survived what is even today an extremely delicate operation. Three hundred and seventy such skulls have been found in Europe, but the finest examples come from Peru. The very thought of thousands—or even millions—of early humans voluntarily submitting to having holes bored in their skulls with primitive flint instruments is enough to make anyone's flesh crawl.

Some anthropologists speculate that trephination was used as a treatment to get rid of possessing spirits. But the universality of this very sophisticated operation makes this unlikely.

Were all those people seeking to open the door in their heads so they could communicate with the supernatural? If so, who or what taught the entire human race this process? And why?

In legend after legend from every part of the world we are told that early man was primitive and stagnant until the appearance of the god-kings. These mysterious beings introduced writing, laws, agriculture, and perhaps even the rudiments of stone building and medicine. The early peoples were so impressed and so grateful that they dedicated much of their time and effort to preserving images of the god-kings in great statues, temples, and monuments. In fact, many cultures left nothing behind except religious artifacts and carvings lovingly detailing their encounters with the gods.

Identical beliefs appeared simultaneously in all parts of the world. Identical forms of writing suddenly came into practice among cultures completely isolated from each other. The Egyptians were not the only ones who believed that the human body would one day be resurrected whole and that therefore all earthly possessions should be buried with it. Ancient tombs in China, Siberia, and South America were also filled with relics for a future life. How did this relatively complex concept spread to the four corners of the earth?

Even the earliest of men were not so stupid that they could sustain a belief century after century without some kind of evidence to support it. Nor would they be so stupid as to expend their energies, materials, and talents building great monuments to those beliefs without such evidence. Yet the reasonably sophisticated peoples of India and Greece believed wholeheartedly in their gods for thousands of years. Their records demonstrate that these gods appeared frequently before mortal men, taught them, tricked them, offered them hope and faith, and cultivated their religions and beliefs. Temples were erected on the spots where the gods had stood from Stonehenge to Delphi. Often the percipients were instructed to build a temple on this spot. Gold (atomic number—79) has always played an important role in all religions, and most religious buildings are roofed with gold leaf from Buddhist temples to Muslim mosques and Christian cathedrals. Could it be that the mysterious rays of the ancients are somehow able to adjust more easily to the frequency of gold? On holy days a great part of the world's population gathers under these golden roofs to pray and meditate and perhaps to have their minds probed by some invisible concentration of energy.

The modern cults and sciences have seized upon the god-king legends to support their own beliefs and conclusions. Atlantologists prefer to think that Quetzalcoatl and his kin were really from Atlantis. The ufologists have churned out scores of books based on the premise that spacemen visited earth and gave mankind a helping hand in those distant days. It is quite true that the Kachina Clan and most of the other parahumans claimed some relationship to other worlds and far-off stars, particularly the Pleiades.

In all these legends there is another persistent theme: that the god-kings mated with mortal women, impregnated them, and thus started a royal lineage. Tradition claims that the bluebloods of royalty actually had blue blood in their veins in early history, perhaps as a result of this crossbreeding. Even today some royal families suffer from hemophilia. Their blood lacks the ability to coagulate and even a small cut becomes a serious wound. The mating of ordinary women with supernatural beings is an integral part of all religious lore. It is emphasized in the Bible.

Some modern rulers, such as the Emperor of Japan, still claim their family can be traced all the way back to a god-like ancestor. The pharaoh system in Egypt could have begun in this fashion with the parahuman leader of the early Egyptians turning his rule over to a human offspring. By 1000 B.C. most of the god-kings had withdrawn, presumably going off to their legendary mountain hideaways. Their followers assumed, however, that their human descendants were equally wise and possessed of magical powers. Being human, these fallible kings often exploited the fears and beliefs of their people. The later pharaohs successfully masqueraded as gods for centuries. The earth had been divided up by the god-kings, each ruling, even owning, a specific area. This ownership was passed on to the human heirs, and for thousands of years a few dozen families literally owned the entire planet. They intermarried and managed to keep the system going until modern times. Although the king system degenerated slowly, it did not really collapse until 1848.

The god-kings did not put all their eggs in one basket. They established parallel systems of communication and control by establishing priesthoods and strange secret cults and societies whose main purpose was to perpetuate their esoteric teachings. But again the flaws in man's basic character eventually surfaced. Greed and the lust for power caused some of these groups to exploit the populaces. There were periods in history when some of these priesthoods and societies even gained political control in Egypt and elsewhere. It is probable that this happened in the burgeoning South American cultures and may even have led to the downfall of some of them.

A key claim of the early priesthoods was their purported ability to consult with the ultraterrestrials through the use of special plates, amulets, and crystals handed down to them. These artifacts were usually worn about the head and heart during religious ceremonies. In the apocryphal Protevangelion we are told that Joachim, father of the Virgin Mary, visited a priest and said, "'If the Lord be propitious to me, let the plate which is on the priest's forehead make it manifest.' And he consulted the plate the priest wore and saw it and behold, sin was not found in him." Such a plate is described in Exodus 28:36.

Early kings and dictators purportedly consulted with angels and supernatural beings who appeared frequently to advise them. Historical records assert that everyone from Julius Caesar to Napoleon had meetings with mysterious parahumans who materialized and dematerialized mysteriously. The Sacred Crown of St. Stephen is supposed to have been delivered by an angel to a pope who permitted Stephen I to be crowned King of Hungary with it in 1001.

The mysterious Gypsies sometimes claim their amulets and crystal balls were given to them by ultraterrestrials. Numerous modern flying saucer contactees display tektites and pieces of quartz that they say were given to them by Venusians. Mr. Ralph Lael, a businessman in North Carolina who once ran for Congress, visited a cavern deep in Brown Mountain under the auspices of the space people, he says, and was later flown to Venus. He was given some chunks of crystal as proof of his claims.

When Joseph Smith dictated the *Book of Mormon* to his wife, he sat behind a screen with the gold plates, apparently translating them with the crystalline devices he had found in the stone box.

Modern UFO contactee writings are filled with enigmatic statements about crystals and how they hold some key to the mysteries of the universe. There are many interpretations of such statements, but no one has managed to crack their true meaning. In the past fifty years, however, crystals have suddenly assumed great importance to our technology. We call them transistors. Although Pauwels and Bergier shrug off the UFO mystery in their *Morning of the Magicians*, they seem to subscribe to the cultist belief that spacemen representing a superior technology once visited the earth. They offer their charming Cargo Cult Theory, speculating that early man's religious rites were actually based upon their observations of the strange behavior of the god-kings. A god-king manipulated a radio and talked into a stick (microphone). Presto! A fleet of aerial vehicles soon arrived with supplies. After the departure of the god-kings, men tried to imitate them by chanting into sticks too, and so prayer was born.

This brings us full circle. The ultraterrestrials imitated the appearance of man, and eventually man began to imitate them in his rites and ceremonies. We made masks and costumes duplicating their strange appearance. We hauled enormous rocks hundreds of miles and carved replicas of their features for our temples and cities. Whole civilizations of stone builders apparently committed themselves entirely to the service of the god-kings and willingly sacrificed thousands of their own people in bloody ceremonies on the sacred hilltops in tribute to these beings.

For many centuries human sacrifices played an important role in the religions of all the peoples of the earth. In the Bible animal sacrifices are described. Even Abraham led his son to a mountain and prepared to kill him in sacrifice to the *Elohim* (the original biblical word, which is plural and means "gods"; it has been given singular translation in the modern Bible). The early priesthoods wielded considerable power. Oracles and mediums resided in the great temples, issuing accurate prophecies (and many inaccurate ones). It was a time of miracles and magic. The priests were the only educated men and as usual some were unscrupulous enough to turn a neat profit from the beliefs of the people.

But gradually the old tried-and-true methods for communicating with the ultraterrestrials began to fail. According to legend, there was great rivalry among the gods. False messengers betrayed the believers and caused all kinds of mischief. And around 500 B.C. a new force began to make its presence felt among men.

In India a wealthy young man named Siddhartha Gautama fell asleep under a tree, so the story goes, and when he awoke, he was filled with a great new philosophy—a new view of man's relationship to the cosmos. He renounced all his worldly goods and set forth to preach under the name of Buddha.

Around that same time a Persian named Zoroaster underwent a similar experience and founded a great religion. While in far-off China the great philosopher Lao-Tzu created Taoism and reshaped the thinking of the Orient along with another contemporary, Confucius. In the Middle East several of the biblical prophets, including Zachariah and Daniel, were conversing with supernatural entities and undergoing illuminating experiences. None of these men knew that the others even existed. Many centuries would pass before their independent ideas and teachings would spread and even overlap. Yet in time these men, all contemporaries between 600 and 500 B.C., changed the philosophical and theological structure of the civilized world. Because of them that century stands as a landmark in the history of our planet.

So the old priesthoods deteriorated, some were slaughtered outright, and new beliefs were born. These beliefs centered around the awareness that there was some force beyond the ultraterrestrials; that mankind was only part of a larger pattern; and that individuals were merely an extension of some distant, unknown intelligence. The stage was being set for a new conflict, a battle royal between the old gods and this Cosmic Consciousness. Muhammad appeared a thousand years later to lead the Arab people away from the old gods, rallying his people with the chant, "There is but one God, and that God is Allah."

Instead of simply disappearing under the wave of monotheism, the old priesthoods went underground, becoming secret societies devoted to preserving the teachings of the elementals and the secrets of communication.

There was already a tangled maze of such societies, such as the Druids mentioned earlier, so the ultraterrestrials had plenty of followers even into the newly enlightened age.

The Romans were still worshipping their gods on Mount Olympus, and the Hebrews were firm in their belief of Jehovah. Then one day three expensively robed gentlemen with Oriental features strode into the court of King Herod and informed him that a most remarkable child was about to be born somewhere in Judea. Meanwhile the angel Gabriel visited Mary and told her she was to bear this child. The three Orientals made their way to Bethlehem, "accompanied by a brilliant glowing object in the sky."

Joseph left Mary in a cave, according to the Protevangelion, while he went to seek a midwife to help with the birth. Then time stood still! Chapter 8 of the Protevangelion relates:

"But as I was going [said Joseph], I looked up into the air, and I saw the clouds astonished, and the fowls of the air stopping in the midst of their flight. And I looked towards the earth and saw a table spread and working people sitting around it, but their hands were upon the table, and they did not move to eat. They who had meat in their mouths did not eat. And they who lifted them up to their mouths did not put anything in, but all their faces were fixed upwards. And I beheld sheep dispersed and yet the sheep stood still. And the shepherd lifted up his hand to smite them, and his hand continued up. And I looked unto a river and saw the kids with their mouths close to the water and touching it, but they did not drink."

Unbelievable though it may be, this paralysis of time is common in UFO and psychic lore. It is almost as if the world is frozen like a frame of a movie film projected on a screen. Time continues to flow only for the percipient.

When Joseph returned to the cave with a midwife, they found it filled with blinding light. The Christ child was born.

The birth, life, and death of Christ had been prophesied earlier. Brethren of the Qumran priesthood even established a regular night watch, scanning the skies of Judea in expectation of some sign of the heavens. Although the exact birth date of Christ remains a controversy, theologians and scholars believe that it was sometime in the year 4 B.C. That year, according to the astrological records of the Qumran priests, "a comet produced a spectacle," and there was a fiery conjunction of planets in the zodiacal sign of Pisces. Pragmatists assume that the Star of Bethlehem was that comet, and to followers of Velikovsky, it might have been Venus.

Jesus' appointed role seems to have been to try to lure the Hebrews away from Jehovah to worship the supermind of the cosmos, the God of the Oriental Illumined Ones. In this he failed. The Jews had had considerable experience with miracles and false angels, and they viewed Christ with great suspicion. The Romans who occupied Judea were still worshiping their assortment of long-haired deities, so they also frowned upon the activities of this persuasive man. However, the sequence of events surrounding the death of Christ provided proof to sway many into Christian beliefs and lay the foundation for the great Christian religions.

An eclipse of the sun threw the land into darkness as Christ hung suspended on the cross. A violent earthquake that claimed many lives followed. Pontius Pilate, the Roman governor of Judea, later collected the witnesses of these events and had them dictate to scribes what they had seen. This record was sent on to Rome. Pilate eventually committed suicide.

The body of Christ was placed in a cave, according to historical records, and a huge stone was rolled in place to seal the entrance. Roman guards were stationed there to keep watch. They testified later:

> There was a great voice in the heavens, and they saw the heavens open, and two men descend from thence with great light and approach the tomb. And that stone which was put at the door rolled of itself and made way in part; and the tomb was opened, and both young men entered in. When therefore those soldiers saw it, they awakened the centurion and the elders; for they too were hard by keeping guard. And as they had seen, again they see three men come forth from the tomb, and two of them were supporting one and a cross following them.

In other texts these two young men were described as wearing brilliantly white costumes, and the soldiers were reportedly paralyzed "like dead men," unable to move a muscle, while the body of Christ was being removed. Later "the heavens again were seen to open, and a certain man to descend and enter the sepulcher."

This certain man remained behind, for when the soldiers and followers of Christ approached the tomb, this being told them not to be frightened and advised them that Christ had been taken or had risen.*

Here we have an extraordinary sequence of events and coincidences. Natural catastrophes struck the exact area where Christ died. A group of witnesses heard a sound in the sky, saw a brilliant light, and were rendered immobile as two beings descended, entered the tomb, and removed the body. One entity remained behind *to make sure* that everyone knew what had happened. Later the ghost of Christ appeared before his disciples to further explain the concept of resurrection. A concept which, as has already been pointed out, can be traced back to the early Egyptian civilization.

Christ's ministry was brief, spanning only a few years, He traveled only a few hundred miles and spoke to only a few thousand people. Nevertheless, his impact upon human history is undeniable and immeasurable. Buddha and Lao-Tzu changed the whole texture of life in the Orient, then five hundred years later Christ wrought a similar change the West.

A series of minor miracles, visitations, and supernatural manifestations reinforced the beliefs of the early Christians, and they willingly died in the Roman circuses for those beliefs. Then gradually the pure Christian concepts absorbed into the established god-king system. A succession of religious wars swept the West, claiming the lives of millions. Opportunists and exploiters moved in as the Roman Empire collapsed (about A.D. 476), and the Dark Ages began. The biblical records were suppressed, censored, and distorted. Various churches openly controlled the kings of Europe and manipulated political affairs. By this time mankind had been misled so often by false

---

*Sources include: The Gospel of Nicodemus: X; The Lost Gospel According to Peter: Verses 9–13; Upton Clary Ewing, *The Prophet of the Dead Sea Scrolls;* and Dr. Hugh Schonfield, *The Report of Pontius Pilate, Governor of Judea, to Tiberius Caesar in Rome* and *The Passover Plot.* The same story, very abridged, is found in the Bible: St. Matthew: 28; St. Mark: 16; St. Luke: 24; and St. John: 20.

prophets and mischievous ultraterrestrials that new encounters on any level were harshly dealt with. When Joan of Arc (1412–31) rallied the French people under guidance of supernatural voices during the Hundred Years' War, she was accused of sorcery and burned at the stake.

Radical developments in science and philosophy that ran contrary to the accepted cosmologies of the time were regarded as the work of the devil. Galileo was imprisoned for daring to suggest that the earth revolved around the sun.

European conquerors and missionaries went off to Africa, Asia, and the Americas, wantonly destroying whole civilizations (such as the Incas) and deliberately disposing of their ancient records. Great nations were plundered for gold. Great and noble cultures were obliterated. A large part of man's past was forever wiped away. It was humanity's darkest hour.

But despite the terror of the inquisitions and the vicious oppression by the monarchies, the secret cults and societies survived, and fragments of the ancient teachings and beliefs were preserved. The day of the alchemist was at hand. It finally came with stunning velocity in the nineteenth century.

Chapter Thirteen

The Secret of the Ages

DOES YOUR NEXT DOOR NEIGHBOR make strange noises behind drawn shades late at night? Have you ever seen him wandering across a darkened cemetery dressed in a robe, carrying a candle? Maybe he is just plain crazy. Then again, maybe he is a member of one of the thousands of secret societies and cults which still flourish everywhere on this haunted planet. If these cults were a permanent part of the human condition it is highly unlikely that Neil Armstrong and Buzz Aldrin would have left their footprints on the moon. And it is equally unlikely that we would have been able to watch the event on a screen painted with moving electrons in our living rooms.

Many of the true secret cults are founded or designed to conjure up unearthly entities. Over the centuries various fugitives and defectors from these hidden organizations have published fragments of these rites and beliefs. There are hundreds of fascinating books available which spell out these strange truths. In addition, there is a wealth of so-called inspired literature purportedly dictated by the entities themselves or produced through automatic writing. The previously mentioned *Oahspe* is one such book and was typed by a New York dentist, Dr. John Ballou Newbrough, in 1880. It is an enormous work, offering a history of the human race plus a complicated cosmology that amazingly has proven to be at least partially valid. It describes, for example, the Van Allen Belt, a belt of radiation encircling the earth that was not discovered until the advent of man-made satellites. It also contains long chapters describing prehistoric secret societies.

There are isolated groups of rather paranoid researchers making a hobby of investigating secret societies. Foremost of these are the superbuffs who believe that a supergovernment runs the entire world. The death rate of these researchers is unreasonably high, so their paranoia is understandable. Factions of the superbuffery overlap into ufology, the John Birch Society, and the assassination investigators. All fringe groups seem to overlap, even though they tend to ignore, and are even opposed to, each other.

Each secret society has its own vocabulary and explanations. Each has developed a system of lessons and degrees to educate its members slowly and lead them upward to cosmic truth. Some of these organizations are dedicated to the devil and his work. Others are oriented and aim at acquiring a closer relationship with God. The Orient is filled with such groups, from the esoteric cultists in the Himalayas to the assassins of Persia and India. Advanced members these groups allegedly possess powers of telepathic projection. The lamas of Tibet supposedly whip up thought forms and elementals at will through sheer force of mind.

The Gypsies have a secretive habit of congregating on hilltops to meet and converse with materializations. The Voodoo rites of Africa and Haiti also call upon such entities. In Voodoo demonic possession seems to be commonplace, and the zombie myths may have a solid basis in fact. Evil entities are supposedly called forth by Voodoo priests to perform sinister deeds. Papa Duvalier, the late President of Haiti, maintained power by fostering the belief that he directly controlled the Voodoo elementals. Witch doctors of Africa and Juju practitioners in South America are also credited with the ability to summon up ultraterrestrials and put them to work.

But the process works in reverse too, with the entities controlling their masters. The literature on secret societies describes many materializations of fearsome demons who frequently gave out orders, directing the cultists to commit acts of murder and political subversion. To disobey meant death, either at the hands of fellow members or the entity itself. Thus the ultraterrestrials are presumably able to guide and control human events through evil men lusting for power.

A young Jordanian in California, Sirhan Sirhan, studied the Rosicrucian doctrines of inspired treatments of mysticism. He practiced self-hypnosis and automatic writing, perhaps hoping to find a way to power and prestige.

In any case, he ended up in a hotel kitchen with a smoking pistol in his hand and Sen. Robert F. Kennedy stretched out at his feet. At his trial Sirhan claimed he had no memory of that fateful night after he entered the hotel. Witnesses said they had seen him talking briefly with a swarthy man who may have been a Mexican or an Oriental. While sitting in the courtroom, Sirhan spoke quietly of seeing celestial beings.

Fire usually plays an important role in secret rites. Rosicrucians practice staring at a candle flame, trying to make the flame obey their will. In the rites of witchcraft—according to the witch hunters—the devil was said to materialize in a bonfire, stepping forward to have sexual intercourse with the witches.

Sex is heavily intermixed with cultist rites and beliefs, particularly in black magic. Moon Children are supposed to be produced when the devil or assorted demons have intercourse with human females. Apparently John Parsons and L. Ron Hubbard tried to produce a Moon Child in 1946. Aleister Crowley fired off an angry letter to the head of the American magick cult, saying, "Parsons or Hubbard or somebody is producing a Moon Child. I get fairly frantic when I contemplate the idiocy of these louts." According to legend, Moon Children grow into exceptionally evil adults with extraordinary powers. (This does not apply, of course, to astrological Moon Children born under the sign of Cancer, June 22-July 22.)

In ufological lore there exist several reports from different parts of the world describing how young men were taken aboard flying saucers and invited to have sexual intercourse with blond spacewomen with long fingers and Oriental features. This appears to be a variation of the Moon Children and succubus phenomenon so well known in religious and occult lore.

The reverse of this is the equally well-known incubus, or demon lover, who forces his attentions on sleeping females. There are UFO cases of this also. A California schoolteacher, Cordelia Donovan, claims that in 1966 she met a man in a long white robe who kidnapped her in a black Cadillac and gassed her. When she awoke, she was aboard a flying saucer, where she was raped by a well-endowed spaceman.* There are innumerable rumors of space

---

*The full details of her incredible story are related by Jan Hudson, *Those Sexy Saucer People*.

babies being born in England, Australia, South America, Mexico, and the United States. Such stories have had great impact on some UFO cultists, who fear that the flying saucer fiends are engaged in a massive biological experiment—creating a hybrid race that will eventually take over the earth.

Theologians and psychiatrists have been trying to cope with the incubus-succubus phenomena for years, but no reasonable medical or psychological explanation has been developed. Many cases can be found in the psychiatric and occult literature, and author Brad Steiger cites dozens in his two books, *Sex and the Supernatural* and *Haunted Lovers*.

The long-fingered, blond elementals have intruded into every aspect of human existence, even including sex. Male and female cultists have apparently been submitting their persons to these lascivious spirits for millennia. They came to us first with the flutter of angels' wings. Now they rape us aboard flying saucers. The game remains the same, only the outward trappings have changed.

Rites to rouse these elementals have endured century after century. If they didn't work, they would have eventually been abandoned. Apparently they do work for somebody...and those who have results write more forbidden books to perpetuate the practices.

There is black magic and white magic. The black magicians supposedly control, or are controlled by, evil entities. The white magicians summon up angels and good guys. Tradition has it that the two groups have been in continual conflict throughout history, constantly waging magical war upon one another.

One of the standard rites for materializing an angel requires the services of a child aged six to eight. An altar is set up, candles are lighted, the child kneels, and the magician chants certain prayers meant to call up the invisible forces around us. The ceremony is repeated for three days near an open window. The elemental is said to appear at the window in a blaze of light, and magicians are warned not to get too close lest they come down with nausea, actinic burns, and other *ailments identical to those reported by low-level UFO witnesses.*

The descriptions of the gods of the ancient world often included similar warnings. It was supposed to be dangerous, if not fatal, to look directly at a god. Perhaps because some of these materializations are composed of pure electromagnetic energy and radiate massive doses of X-rays, gamma rays, and ultraviolet rays. Such rays would produce the above medical effects. Conjunctivitis, an inflammation of the eyes, is a commonly observed effect among UFO witnesses.

Both the literature of the secret societies and the more readily available general occult literature warn about the hazards of these practices. Poorly informed, emotionally unstable practitioners can be overwhelmed by the forces they unleash. The blundering amateur wizard can become possessed or driven insane or experience elaborate hallucinations for extended periods. All kinds of weird manifestations can descend on him, ranging from poltergeists to violent physical attacks by invisible hands. These classic psychic attacks are very similar to the problems suffered by some innocent UFO witnesses and contactees after their sightings begin. The two phenomena seem to be inexorably linked.

Modern science, with its obsession about the physical universe and the physical laws that run it, is only about three hundred years old. Eighty percent of all the scientists who ever lived are living at this moment, although, in truth, most of them are technologists and engineers rather than pure scientists. But that's a point too minor to debate. Science was successfully suppressed throughout the Dark Ages and even into the seventeenth century (remember Galileo). But another kind of science did exist.

The science of magic.

Ironically, magical beliefs of the past five thousand years are based upon the same principles that rule modern scientific thought: the study of atomic structure and electromagnetic energy. Astrology, the forerunner of astronomy, was a highly advanced science thousands of years ago. Some of the ancient calendars and records are so accurate and so detailed that there has been speculation that the ancient astrologers may have had telescopes and other sophisticated instruments. If they didn't, then they must have received some help and guidance from someone who understood the structure of the universe. The early astrologers were, of course, priests and magicians. They systematically cataloged the visible objects in the heavens, naming them and interpreting their influence on man and human events. Astrology became the first mathematical science.

While the astrologers were putting mathematics to work, other men were delving into the mysteries of the physical planet earth, cataloging metals, elements, and chemicals and learning how to combine them into new forms. They were the alchemists: the sorcerers' apprentices. They dreamed of finding some way of turning lead into gold. During some periods in history the alchemists were supported by kings, while in other periods they were the victims of superstitious purges which forced them underground. Their secret societies preserved and circulated hundreds of manuscripts that were half science and half mysticism. Many alchemists first entered the field after encounters with ultraterrestrials and became the proud, if furtive, predecessors of men like Cyrus Teed.

Men who were students of astrology, alchemy, and magic all at once served as the educated elite during long periods of history, acting as priests, scientists, and educators. Some of them also belonged to another elite group, the master stonemasons, and they were able to put their polyglot knowledge to work by designing the great stone monuments and engineering the methods by which they were built. In time these master stonemasons formed a fraternity to preserve their occult secrets and to assist one another as they wandered from place to place seeking work. This was the beginning of the Masonic order. As the centuries passed, the fraternity expanded to include businessmen, educators, and leaders.

Although the modern Masonic movement is looked upon with some suspicion by the various buff groups, the ufologists delight in pointing out that most of the men who signed the Declaration of Independence were Masons, as was Joseph Smith, founder of the Mormon religion. Masonic lore has found its way into many of our governmental symbols and institutions, including the Great Seal of the United States, which bears the slogan *Novus Ordo Seclorum*, "A New Order for the Ages." The design for the Great Seal is supposed to have been handed to Thomas Jefferson in his garden one night by a mysterious stranger dressed in a cape with a hood over his head.

The superbuffs have scuffled through history books to try to pinpoint the origin and location of the fabled supergovernment and the identities of its members. One group believes they are key industrialists (particularly munitions makers) and bankers. Others have produced dozens of books advocating anti-Semitism and claiming that a secret inner circle of Jews has been working for generations on a plan to take over the world. One of the most vicious and most successful racist books ever written came out of Russia in the last century and is called *The Protocols of the Elders of Zion*. This obvious hoax purports to be the Jewish master plan for gaining control of the world's gold and the press. Oddly enough, Adolf Hitler seems to have used the *Protocols* as a guidebook in his bid for power. Jewish cultists have fought back with their claim that a Catholic conspiracy exists. Jesuit priests are a favorite target of this group. It is a fact that the Jesuits (the Society of Jesus) engaged in so many political conspiracies in the eighteenth century that the Vatican was compelled to dissolve the order in 1773. It was reestablished in 1814. Today the order is largely confined to running schools such as Georgetown University in Washington, D.C.

Following World War II, men like J. Edgar Hoover and the late Sen. Joseph McCarthy gave impetus to the public paranoia over the Communist Conspiracy. This was partly based upon the spread of left wing beliefs during the social unrest of the 1930s, when intellectuals and workingmen embraced, temporarily, the Communist ideology. It was based partly upon Joseph Stalin's mad machinations in the early days of the Cold War. The gradual thaw that followed Stalin's death and the public revelations of his outrageous purges ultimately broke the Communist Party in the United States. The numerous organizations and buff groups that had been dedicated to combating the partly real and partly illusory Communist threat began to flounder and look around for a new cause.

They found it when, in his final speech as president, Dwight Eisenhower issued a guarded warning about the growth of what he termed "the military-industrial complex." The assorted buff groups scurried back to the earlier literature on the supergovernment. They extended Ike's warning to include religion and came up with the religious-military-industrial conspiracy—a plot against humanity that supposedly included the churches (notably the Catholic church), the Pentagon, and the huge industries that were churning out weapons that have never been used.

By the end of the 1960s our social and political problems had generated a whole maze of new supposed conspiracies. The extreme right and left wings found themselves in the absurd position of advocating the same beliefs and fears. Everything from sex education to the fluoridation of water became an issue within the context of their beliefs. As they stumbled about searching for a new explanation behind the universal madness, many of these groups, ranging from the John Birch Society to our youth subculture—the hippie movement—rediscovered the Illuminati. The Communist Conspiracy was nearly forgotten as everyone went after the Illuminati.

Do the Illuminati even exist? It is very unlikely. The buff groups have confused some of the earlier secret societies with the process of mystical illumination. Illumined individuals, like water, tend to seek their own level and associate with their own kind. Often they withdraw from society altogether, the ascetics of India being one example.

There is another form of pseudo-illumination, however, which is actually a form of demonic possession and frequently produces religious fanatics. A majority of all the political assassinations in history were committed by victims of this. John Wilkes Booth and his nine fellow conspirators are a prime example, as were Leon Czolgosz, who gunned down President McKinley in 1901; the young student who assassinated Archduke Franz Ferdinand of Austria in 1914, thus launching World War I; and Benjamin Mendoza y Amor, the Bolivian artist who attacked Pope Paul with a knife on November 26, 1970. Witnesses said that the latter would-be assassin "looked like he was having an epileptic fit"—one of the classic symptoms of possession.

Some buff groups regard these maniacal killers as tools of the sinister Illuminati who have been pressed into service by hypnosis or some other brainwashing technique. They are quick to point out that Jack Ruby pulled his gun and shot down Lee Harvey Oswald after being triggered by an auto horn that suddenly beeped in the basement of the Dallas police station. (No one has ever determined who blew that horn or why.) Ruby claimed to his dying day that he had no memory of entering the police station or firing the shot.

Like many major myths, the Illuminati legend began in the Orient. Around 275 B.C. Asoka, the Emperor of India, is supposed to have founded the super-secret society of the Nine Unknown Men. This group was founded to collect, study, and protect the secrets of the occult, science, alchemy, astrology, and psychology. As late as 1927 Talbot Mundy, a specialist in Oriental lore, was writing about the mysterious Nine, implying that the society still existed and was still running things from far behind the scenes.

In the tenth century young men were enticed into Persia's cult of the assassins by drugs and beautiful young ladies. Founded by Sabah, the old man of the mountains who was purportedly one of the mystic Nine, the cult conducted a reign of terror that continued into this century. It may in fact still exist. They had tremendous political influence during various periods of history. The brainwashed, drugged members of the cult carried out their orders blindly, even when those orders were suicidal.

A similar cult appeared in Afghanistan in the sixteenth century. This was known as the Roshaniya—the Illuminated Ones. Like the Hashishim assassin cult of Persia, the Roshaniya appears to have been inspired by a prophet in communication with the ultraterrestrials. It began as a mystical order that quickly degenerated into a band of blind, drugged, mentally controlled murderers. They raised a lot of hell in Afghanistan for several generations, and their secret teachings spread into Europe. The Alumbrados—the Illuminated Ones of Spain—appeared around 1600. In France the Guerinets, another branch of the Illuminati, caused some excitement in 1654. A professor of canon law at Ingolstadt University in Bavaria, Adam Weishaupt, founded the German Illuminati in the seventeenth century.

One of the stated purposes of the Illuminati was to take over the world and establish a New Order that was basically antireligious. They wanted to get rid of the archaic god-king system and all the tyranny that went along with it. This was naturally a very unpopular concept with the established authorities, and great efforts were made to track down and execute the members of the cult. By the late 1700s the movement had been effectively crushed.

And the persistent legend of the Illuminati was born.

They tried at one point to infiltrate and take over the Freemasons, and this gave rise to the still prevalent belief (in some quarters) that the Masons are actually a wing of the Illuminati. Following the American Revolution a vast amount of literature appeared claiming that the United States was actually part of the Illuminati Plot and had been founded by secret members of the cult. The Bill of Rights was in fact a very radical document for the period with its insistence that all men are created equal, that there should be freedom of religion, and that the affairs of man should be governed by men elected to office. The Illuminati Conspiracy attracted the same kind of attention in the early 1800s as the Communist Conspiracy did in the 1950s.

A French book, *La Secte des Illuminés,* published in the 1790s, presented a description of the Illuminati initiation rites:

> On the day of his initiation, the candidate was conducted through a long, dark passage into an immense hall draped with black…Ghostly forms moved through the hall, leaving behind them a foul odor…His clothes were removed and laid upon a funeral pyre. Then his pudenda [genitals] were tied with string…Now five horrid and frightening figures, bloodstained and mumbling, approached him and threw themselves down in prayer. After an hour sounds of weeping were heard, the funeral pyre started to burn, and his clothes were consumed. From the flames of this fire a huge and almost transparent form arose, while the five prostrate figures went into terrible convulsions. Now came the voice of an invisible hierophant [priest], booming from somewhere below…

This was of course a typical magical rite—the rousing of an elemental. Most of the secret cults of ancient and modern times are centered around such rites. Most of them have preserved the same truths throughout history with numerous variations. These same truths were accepted by all the assorted priesthoods and religious orders also, and all the early kings were trained to understand and accept them. They also formed the basis for the sciences of astrology, alchemy, witchcraft, and black magic. Terminology differed from group to group; each had a different label for the various aspects, but they all believed—and still believe—in these basic supernatural facts.

The first and most important secret that has been carefully guarded and withheld from the public at large is that two or more worlds exist, composed of different forms of matter but occupying the same space. Part of the teachings of all cults includes elaborate definitions of these different forms of matter. When the nonsensical terms are translated into modern terminology, it is apparent that these teachings are concerned with advanced physics, nuclear energy, atomic structure, and things that have only recently been discovered by modern science. Electrical energy is also discussed at great length in terms of vibrations, and this material can be easily translated into contemporary terms of wave lengths and frequencies. Ancient man knew that smashing the atom yields pure energy. He knew that human eyes could only see a tiny portion of the electromagnetic spectrum (visible light), and he believed that other worlds or realities existed beyond the limitations of his sight.

Specter, the ancient word for ghostly apparition, sprang from *spectrum.* Early peoples observed that these objects or entities were able to reflect or cast off light wavelengths from the entire visible spectrum from violet at one end to red at the other. They knew they were seeing transmogrifications of electrical energy. Countless modern UFO reports describe these same color changes. UFOs often appear first as a purplish blob and then descend the visible scale until they turn red, at which point they sometimes solidify into seemingly material objects. This process is fully explored in the ancient literature.

Dualism, particularly stressed in the Orient, separates the world of the mind from the world of the physical. It is believed that the human mind and consciousness are merely a part of a larger universal mind and that with proper training and study we can learn to tap that universal mind. On the simplest level the masses try to do this with prayer. On the more esoteric level of the cults it is taught that the mind can be made powerful enough to manipulate atomic energy and thus control the material world. One of the great secrets is that if a man can learn to visualize, say a chair, and can form every atom of that chair in his imagination, he can actually cause a physical chair to materialize. Or working in reverse, he can dematerialize a physical object. Such thought forms even include animated entities. So the rites of magic are aimed at concentrating the energy of human minds on a specific point in space and literally wishing a being to appear. In theory the minds would be forcing electrical energy to assume visible, physical form.

The infringement of the other worlds beyond the visible is the cornerstone of occult belief. The inhabitants of those other dimensions can supposedly manipulate energy much more easily than we can. They can enter our dimension or reality and assume temporary physical form. Some can do this on their own. Others require the assistance of human minds before they can materialize. The secret cults have happily supplied this service for thousands of years. Today there is a worldwide revival of witchcraft. Some American high schools and colleges are even conducting courses in witchcraft. The ultraterrestrials must be having a field day!

Early man was quite convinced that these invisible worlds existed. This led him to the secret of the ages: the belief that mankind was actually controlled by the inhabitants of these other planes or dimensions. The modes of control became the chief concern of the cultists, magicians, and priesthoods. Political and religious structures were set up to facilitate that control, as we have already pointed out.

Dr. Gordon Allen, an aerospace scientist, summarized a lifetime of study into these matters in his book, *Enigma Fantastique:*

The purpose today is identical to the purpose in the times of the magician-scientists of ancient times, the purpose of the controlling priesthood of the Egyptians, the Caesars, the Roman Catholic church, the Inquisition. The ecclesiastic control of the various ruling families had for its purpose the rule of the people in their material bodies on this earth-plane.

A nation is said by Eastern philosophers to lie under certain occult (or secret) controls. Nations who go to war on the earth-plane reflect certain wars in Heaven.

It is true that the Masonic founders of the United States knew of this occult control and even something of their own mission. Ruling families of

Europe knew of this occult control and believed themselves in power by divine right, but occult control was secret and not discussed by historians or political writers until just the last few years.

All of this may be absolute nonsense, but we cannot overlook the unhappy fact that these truths were completely believed for thousands of years by the leaders of the world and therefore had an appalling influence over human events and destiny. Bloody religious wars were fought for centuries as the different religions attempted to gain total domination of the known world.

Even worse, man's own record of his early history was systematically destroyed by the conflicting factions. The library at Alexandria, Egypt, which housed thousands of years of history, was sacked and burned. The remnants of early cultures were wantonly destroyed. And then we were given a new history, generously dictated by the ultraterrestrials, and we bogged down in the Dark Ages for a thousand years. The human race quite willingly turned itself over to the ultraterrestrials.

It was not until the nineteenth century that we began to claw our way out from under occult rule. In 1848 the whole world exploded. There were more than fifty major revolutions. Spiritualism was born that year in Wayne County, New York, when two teenaged girls—the Fox sisters—learned to communicate with a rapping poltergeist. The *Communist Manifesto* was published. Kings were dethroned. There were major political assassinations just as mysterious as the murder of President Kennedy. The first Woman's Suffrage Movement got underway in Seneca Falls, New York. The whole world was suddenly in upheaval. A host of brilliant inventors and scientists suddenly appeared simultaneously, and the great Industrial and Scientific Revolutions got underway. (Thomas Edison was born in 1847.) Mankind hurtled into a fantastic hundred-year period that saw the rapid development of steamboats, railroads, airplanes, and finally the atomic bomb. Social structures everywhere were suddenly revised.

Ironically, the feared goals of the seventeenth-century Illuminati have now become a reality to millions of people. Red China and the Soviet Union went to an extreme, suppressing religion and carving out totalitarian states that appeared to be steps towards robotizing the human race.

But the technological advances and the conflict of political ideologies are insignificant when compared to the amazing revolution of the mind that took place almost unnoticed—in the 1960s. The secret cults of the past were replaced by the eerie mysticism of the LSD cults and the hippie movement. Young people everywhere turned to witchcraft and magic and engaged in a sophisticated form of occultism that attempted to link their minds with the Cosmic Consciousness.

It is easy to see why some buffs and cults viewed all this with alarm and tried to blame the mythical Nine Unknown Men or Illuminati. Anyone who studies history carefully can detect the presence of some outside influence—an influence that has largely been detrimental, even sinister. Yet the ancient gods and the modern Brothers from space have come to us in a benevolent guise. They have never practiced what they preached.

To support our outrageous hypothesis we must make two basic assumptions: (1) That the ultraterrestrials are real in some manner and are not merely a psychological phenomenon or myth. (2) That the UTs have a *need* for communicating with us. If such a need exists, then it would be logical for them to create secret societies or even a whole race of people to carry out their wishes. To be truly effective, such a race would have to be clannish and aloof from the societies in which it moved. They would, undoubtedly, be so strange and furtive that outsiders would soon surround them with legends and nonsense.

A group like this *does* exist. They are spread all over the world. We call them Gypsies. The ultimate secret society.

Nobody really knows where the Gypsies come from, not even the Gypsies themselves! Some tribes have advanced the notion that they somehow came from the sky. We do know that no Gypsies existed before their sudden appearance in Europe in the fourteenth century. They identified themselves as Dukes of Egypt. They quickly established themselves as remarkable magicians and clairvoyants and were regarded as the fulfillment of Ezekiel's prophecy, "I shall scatter the Egyptians among the nations." Their talents for sorcery and fortunetelling led to the creation of a whole body of myth. Even the modern Washington seer, Jeane Dixon, claimed that a wandering Gypsy lady presented her with her first crystal ball when she was eight.

Gypsies have their own language, which is derived from Hindi and Tibetan. They apparently have no racial ties with the Egyptians at all but probably came from India and Afghanistan originally. In February 1968, a Gypsy tribe established a government-in-exile in Paris to demand payment of reparations from the Germans for what they suffered in World War II, claiming that four million Gypsies had perished in Hitler's death camps. They also announced their plans to reestablish Romanistan where Somaliland is today. They even sought United Nations recognition.

An estimated two million Gypsies now live in the United States, so they outnumber the surviving Indians by a large margin. But they are a silent minority, remaining by themselves, keeping their children out of public schools and suffering constant persecution without complaint. Gypsies do not use the mails or telephones, yet when a prominent Gypsy dies, the word seems to spread instantly, and tribes from all over the country converge for the funeral. They pay no income taxes, even though some tribes seem to have accrued considerable wealth and ride about in big black Cadillacs.

The Gypsy religion is a curious mixture of witchcraft, black magic, and elementalism. Periodically, all the Gypsies will spring into their Cadillacs in the middle of the night and drive off to some isolated forest or hilltop where, according to reliable sources, they converse with materializations. Gypsies also have a curious habit of turning up in Window areas during UFO flaps.

Morris K. Jessup caused the Gypsies to become part of the UFO lore in the 1950s when he received a series of strange letters from one Carlos Allende. A couple of these letters were released to the UFO buffs and have been a source of controversy ever since. In 1955 a paperback copy of Jessup's *The Case for the UFO* arrived in the mail at the Office of Naval Research (ONR). The pages of the book were covered with marginal notes penciled in by three different hands. These comments indicated that the anonymous writers were extremely knowledgeable in UFO matters and made a number of pointed references that suggested they were Gypsies. Although Jessup himself dismissed the annotations as some kind of hoax, the ONR was so impressed that they had the whole book retyped and reproduced with the marginal notes printed in different colors. The reproduction was prepared for the Navy by the Varo Corporation in Garland, Texas. One of Allende's letters to Jessup, dated January 13, 1956, was postmarked in Gainesville, Texas, which is about sixty miles north of Garland. Only a few hundred copies of this Varo edition were printed, and they were carefully distributed to a select few within the Navy. Since it has always been almost unobtainable, very few UFO buffs have ever even seen this interesting document.

The annotations discuss the Great Ark (which supposedly circles Jupiter and has already been discussed) and try to answer some of the questions Jessup raised in his book. Jessup was found dead in his automobile in Dade County Park near Coral Gables, Florida, on April 20, 1959—an apparent suicide. But Carlos Allende has gone marching on.

A fantastic array of Allende imposters have turned up over the years to bedevil and bewilder the UFO buffs. He has managed to turn up in several different states at the same time. All kinds of letters and phone calls have been received by buffs in his name. Those who claim to have met him describe him as a swarthy man of Cuban or Spanish extraction. He rides around in a black Cadillac, of course. Until the late 1960s, Allende was nothing more than a myth bandied about in the very limited UFO buff circles. Then author Brad Steiger obtained a photostated copy of the Varo edition and used it as the basis of an article in *Saga* magazine. He was instantly inundated with new Allende letters and even a letter from a woman claiming to be Allende's widow.

In 1969 a man claiming to be Carlos Allende visited the Lorenzens, who operated the civilian research group, APRO, in Tucson, Arizona. He presented them with an original copy of the Varo publication. How he managed to acquire the copy was not determined. (The real Allende, if there is a real Allende, would not have had access to a copy.)

Other mystery men of the Allende type have haunted the UFO researchers for years. In the early 1960s a man calling himself Zdeen Alexander toured the United States, amusing some flying saucer enthusiasts and terrifying others. He answered to the usual description. Some buffs claimed he was able to disappear in front of their eyes. He visited prominent ufologists in New

York and offered to finance a newsstand UFO publication. In California he predicted the appearance of UFOs in Santa Barbara, and those predictions came true. After shaking everyone up, he simply dropped from sight.

The next mystery man appeared in Boulder, Colorado, during a Colorado University UFO research project. He arrived in a chaffeur-driven Cadillac, marched straight into the office of Dr. Edward U. Condon, head of the project, and announced that he was Mr. Dixsun and represented the Seventh Universe. He was, of course, a swarthy little man wearing dark glasses. He offered to help Dr. Condon contact the space people, provided he received a substantial amount of money. Condon was not exactly enthused, so Mr. Dixsun got into his Cadillac and drove off to rendezvous with Mr. Alexander and Mr. Allende.

It is likely that some of these characters were actually Gypsies playing some little game of their own. Many of these hoaxes were very complicated and expensive, and the perpetrators obviously had both imagination and a sense of humor. Flying saucer enthusiasts are notably lacking in these qualifications. But why would anyone bother to spend inordinate amounts of time and money contriving and executing elaborate pranks against random cultists?

The answer seems to be that believers have always been dished up manifestations which appeared to support their beliefs. Believe in the devil and he will appear, the old saying goes. An even older saying, dating back to the dawn of history, states that those whom the gods wish to destroy they first make mad.

An ancient madness is overtaking the human race in these closing years of the twentieth century.

"Why don't they contact us?" the skeptics ask.

It might be better for us to ask, "Why didn't they leave us alone?"

Part Three

Alice laughed. "There's no use trying," she said, "one can't believe impossible things."

"I daresay you haven't had much practice," said the Queen. "When I was younger, I always did it for half an hour a day. Why, sometimes I've believed as many as six impossible things before breakfast."

—Lewis Carroll, *Through the Looking Glass*

Chapter Fourteen

"Hello, Control. Give Me Ganymede."

HIGH ON A BLEAK MOUNTAINSIDE six thousand feet above sea level outside of Colorado Springs, Colorado, a weird looking tower jutted 135 feet into the air in the summer of 1899. It was designed and erected by a tall, gaunt man named Nikola Tesla—the now forgotten genius who perfected alternating current and whose many contributions to our electrical age are almost inestimable. Thomas Alva Edison walked away with most of the glory, and Tesla ended up a burnt-out eccentric, alone and ignored in a dingy Manhattan hotel room. But while the spark was in him it shed a blinding glare.

That summer, using thirty thousand dollars given to him by Col. John Jacob Astor, Nikola Tesla was experimenting with radio. He had built a powerful transmitter and receiver and was trying to develop a method for broadcasting electrical energy through the air to eliminate the need for expensive wiring systems. Energy that could run motors and light lamps. He succeeded at least partially, for the lights and equipment in his later laboratories worked without wiring.

Thousands of miles away a young man named Marconi was also toying with batteries and coils. That summer Marconi managed to broadcast the letter V (three dots and a dash) to a crude receiver operated by his assistants less than fifty miles away. These were the only operable radios on the planet earth.

But somewhere there must have been a third transmitter.

One night while Tesla was working alone in his mountain lab, his equipment suddenly came to life, and he received an apparently intelligent signal, though indecipherable. "I was familiar, of course, with such electrical disturbances as are produced by the sun, Aurora Borealis, and earth currents," he later wrote, "and I was as sure as I could be of any fact that these variations were due to none of these causes...The feeling is constantly growing on me that I had been the first to hear the greeting of one planet to another."

Tesla became the first scientist to intercept the mysterious, intelligently organized radio waves which permeate our planet and have baffled generations of scientists. He was a very odd man, sexless and mystical. In 1900 he told a reporter, "We cannot even with positive assurance assert that some of them [ultraterrestrials] might not be present here in this our world in the very midst of us, for their constitution and life manifestations may be such that we are unable to perceive them."

He amplified this in 1921 when *American Magazine* quoted him:

> During my boyhood I suffered from a particular affliction due to the appearances of images, which were often accompanied by strong flashes of light. When a word was spoken, the image of the object designated would present itself so vividly to my vision that I could not tell whether what I saw was real or not...Even though I reached out and passed my hand through the image, it would remain fixed in space.

Two years after Tesla's Colorado experiments, Marconi broadcast the letter S (three dots) across the Atlantic, and a new era of communications was born. From the very beginning radio operators throughout the world received signals which no one could identify or understand. Some of these signals were so strong they seemed to be originating only a mile or two from the receiver, and they drowned out all other signals. The only identifiable thing about these enigmatic messages was the repetitive transmission of the letter V. Marconi reported that stations of his company on both sides of the Atlantic picked up these pirate signals even before World War I. In 1921 Marconi stated flatly that he believed that the signals were coming from another civilization from somewhere in space.

By the time 1924 rolled around signals from Mars were a popular theme in the Sunday supplements, and when the orbit of Mars brought it close to the earth in 1924, a well organized program was set up to intercept any possible transmissions. Most of the major radio stations and ham rigs around the world deliberately fell silent and listened. Dr. David Todd, head astronomer at Amherst College, set up a gadget known as the Jenkins Radio-Camera at a naval observatory. (Jenkins was a pioneer TV experimenter.) Mars crept closer, and everyone waited. On August 24, 1924 (note the date), amateur, military, and government radio stations closed down their transmitters. They were not disappointed. Freak signals of unidentifiable origin were reported by awed listeners all over the world. Dr. Todd's apparatus whirred and clattered, and a long strip of photographic tape poured out of it. When the tape was developed, it displayed "a fairly regular arrangement of dots and dashes along one side," according to the *New York Times*, "but on the other side at almost evenly spaced intervals are curiously jumbled groups, each taking the form of a crudely drawn human face."

The Jenkins device was technically incapable of producing drawings.

This amazing experiment hit the headlines everywhere, and hundreds of amateur radio operators submitted reports of what they themselves had picked up. Since there were very few commercial stations at the time and most amateurs were operating crude, homemade equipment with very limited capabilities, we have another mystery here. Those freak signals had to be exceptionally strong. There was no possibility of a worldwide hoax, yet it did seem that the signals had to be of terrestrial origin. But from where and by whom?

These signals continued to be received throughout the 1920s and 1930s. Dr. Hugh Mansfield Robinson constructed one set of experiments with a set of high-powered receivers in 1921. He received intelligent signals on the thirty-thousand-meter wavelength and Ernst B. Rogers, the engineer in charge of the test, "felt compelled to state that they were of extraterrestrial origin, as there were no sending instruments of that power on earth."

An amateur radio astronomer named Grote Reber reported receiving strong dot-and-dash signals from space in 1939. He had built a thirty-foot dish antenna in Wheaton, Illinois (just outside of Chicago), and said he often listened to the signals for eight hours at a time. They seemed to come from one specific spot in the sky.

Radio astronomy was then in its infancy and signals were being detected from both Venus and Jupiter. But these appeared to be static-like natural phenomena covering a wide part of the band. Professor Hermann Oberth, the German rocket pioneer, worked with radio telescopes and suggested that intelligent signals were coming from the distant stars of Epsilon Eridani and Tau Ceti, both of which are about eleven light years away. He based his calculations on his erroneous assumption that the signals were sporadic (they are constant) and were only received every twenty-two years, thus taking eleven years to go out and another eleven to be returned.

If the true nature of the central phenomenon is electromagnetic, and if the earth is constantly being bathed in rays or beams of energy under intelligent direction, then these manifestations are hardly surprising. These signals could have existed long before we developed the devices necessary to intercept them. Once we had the necessary equipment, the source of the signals adjusted the frequencies so we could hear them. It—or they—are also able to play havoc with our communications at will...and there is evidence that this is happening.

During the ghost-flier wave over northern Europe in the 1930s, isolated people in Norway and Sweden picked up enigmatic broadcasts on their short-wave sets, purportedly the ufonauts chattering back and forth over the airwaves, often in broken Swedish. The Scandinavian press speculated that Germany or the Soviet Union might be responsible for the broadcasts, but no evidence of this ever came to light.

In countless modern UFO cases witnesses have claimed they received strange guttural voices and dot-and-dash signals on car radios, TV sets, and telephones while flying saucers hovered overhead. Citizens Band (CB) radios also have a habit of picking up these signals in flap areas. On many occasions *these voices and sounds have been emitted by loudspeakers that were not turned on or weren't even connected.*

A loudspeaker consists of an electromagnet which vibrates a cone of paper or stiff cloth. When the cone vibrates, it naturally vibrates the air and produces audible sound waves. Theoretically, a beam of electromagnetic energy on a very low frequency (VLF) could activate the magnet.

In January 1954, people throughout the Midwest allegedly heard a strange voice coming from turned-off radios. The voice stated in a dull monotone: "I wish no one to be afraid, although I speak from space. But if you do not stop preparations for war, you will be destroyed." Even stranger, the same kind of message delivered by the same kind of voice was supposedly picked up by the equipment at the London airport that month.

George Hunt Williamson, a self-styled anthropologist, claimed he was present when an amateur radio operator established contact with another world in the summer of 1952. Here's Williamson's account of that experiment:

> This test was of such a nature that if the messages were a hoax, they would have been revealed as such immediately...He sent a question over his transmitter [to the space people], and he received an answer. Without any warning he quickly switched to 160 meters and asked another question. To his surprise an answer was soon forthcoming! Any radioman knows that no power on earth would have enabled any operator to know where he was switching to. Even if Mr. R. had told the other operator that he was going to switch to 160 meters, still they would not have found him on that band until after the question had been asked. And of course, they couldn't have answered the question if they hadn't heard it!

Williamson spent a lot of time probing around the ancient ruins of South America before he suddenly vanished without a trace in the early 1960s.

At a flying saucer buffs' convention in Giant Rock, California, in 1954, one speaker informed the audience:

> The entities of the spaceships and saucers can and do read the mind of a radio operator, exchanging communications. They know when he is several yards from his set and will give him time to reach it before they signal...In one case involving something in the nature of mind reading at a distance, these entities gave the answer to a discussion going on in a room and not taken up or referred to on the radio.

Quite a few amateur radio operators have joined the ranks of the UFO contactees in recent years, perhaps because all night they sit surrounded by equipment radiating powerful magnetic fields which can somehow be utilized by the phenomena. On August 3, 1958, ham operators throughout the United States reportedly picked up a strange broadcast on the seventy-five-meter international band. A male voice claiming to be "Nacoma from the planet Jupiter" warned his listeners that the atomic bomb tests could lead to disaster. He spoke for two-and-a-half hours in English, German, Norwegian, and his own language, described as kind of musical gibberish.

"It was the most powerful signal we picked up," one account said. "There was plenty of time during the broadcast for hundreds to listen in, and radio operators called in friends and neighbors and phoned long distance to relatives in other states."

The Federal Communications Commission later denied any knowledge of the broadcast.

The far-off, far-out planet of Korendor checked in on a warm night in July 1961. An eighteen-year-old radio buff, Bob Renaud, was "browsing around the shortwave bands" in his home in a little town in Massachusetts, when "suddenly from the loudspeaker came a very high pitched beep-beep-beep." He was annoyed by it, he said, and tried unsuccessfully to tune it out. "It stopped," he wrote later, "but was replaced by a soft, warm, crystal clear feminine voice that said, 'Bob, we'd like you to stay on this frequency for a while.'"

This space lady identified herself as Linn-Erri (like the demons and angels of yesteryear, the space people are fond of names containing double letters). Over the months that followed she dictated endless treatises on what was wrong with us and what was right with her world. The Renaud story quickly fell into the pattern of all the earlier contactees. At 2:00 A.M, on the morning of December 22, 1962, a car drove up in front of his house, according to his story, and three rather normal looking men invited him to hop in. They drove him to an isolated field where they demonstrated an antigravity device that lifted a huge boulder a hundred feet in the air. Then they pointed another gadget at it and it disintegrated in a flash. Later they conducted him on a tour of a secret underground UFO base in Massachusetts and even took him for a little jaunt in a flying saucer.

Following the Korendians' instructions, Renaud claims he rebuilt a TV set so that he could receive outer space TV shows. When Linn-Erri's face appeared on the screen, she turned out to be a beautiful blonde, 37–22–36. She appeared to be eighteen or nineteen years old but admitted to being seventy-four, "which in our society is the prime of life." (Renaud's TV set probably operates on the same nonprinciple employed by the celebrated Psionic Machine of Thomas G. Hieronymous that was promoted by *Astounding Science Fiction* for some years. If the parts are removed from the Psionic Machine, it continues to work anyway because it apparently operates on some psychic force, like Ouija boards and dowsing rods do.)

Another ham radio operator was swallowed up by the contactee phenomenon on January 30, 1965. Towards midnight on January 29, George W. Clemins, mayor of Monterey, California, and several other people reportedly saw a brilliantly illuminated spherical object hovering over Monterey Bay. It appeared to slowly descend out of sight on the other side of the bay. Two hours later a forty-five-year-old TV repairman named Sidney Padrick shut down his ham radio rig and decided to take a stroll before going to sleep. On Manresa Beach directly opposite Monterey he heard a loud humming noise and saw a strange machine shaped like "two real thick saucers inverted." He was none too happy about this apparition, he admitted, and so he turned and started to run away.

"Do not be frightened," a voice reportedly boomed from the object. "We are not hostile." Mr. Padrick kept running. "We mean you no harm. You are welcome to come aboard."

Padrick stopped and considered, feeling slightly bewildered and foolish. A door slid open, he said, and he cautiously approached it. The voice urged him on. He stepped into a small room about six by seven feet, where he was greeted by medium-sized man with very pale skin. He had, Padrick noted, a very sharp nose and chin and unusually long fingers. "His hands were very clean. The fingernails looked as if somebody had just given them a manicure." Padrick said:

They wore two-piece suits with no buttons or zippers that I could see. The bottom section actually included shoes—it looked like boots which continued on up to the waistline without any break around the ankles, just like a child's snowsuit. They had soles and heels similar to ours—I could hear them walking with a "thump-thump" sound on the rubbery-like floor. The collar had a very pretty design on it—it came down to a V in the front, and the neckpiece, right around his neck, had a braid of some kind on it, very pretty. It had colors, but I can't tell you what they were, because they weren't colors that I had ever seen before…much more beautiful than ours.

When Padrick asked for the man's name, he was told, "You may call me Zeeno." Although the witness didn't know it, the Greek word for stranger *(xeno)* is pronounced *zee-no.* Being a technician, Padrick was able to supply a detailed description of the interior of the craft and was nonplussed when Mr. Zeeno showed him a room "similar to a chapel."

The color effect in that room was so pretty that I almost fainted when I went in. A mixture of beautiful colors can't describe it. There were eight chairs, a stool, and what appeared to be an altar. Zeeno said, "Would you like to pay your respects to the Supreme Deity?" I didn't know how to accept it…I'm forty-five years old, and until that night I had never felt the presence of the Supreme Being, but I did feel Him that night.

After taking a short flight in the object, Padrick claimed he was returned to the beach where he had been picked up. He reported his experience to the Air Force immediately and was later interviewed for three hours by officers from the nearby Hamilton Air Force Base. "They wanted an account of it, word for word," he said in a later telephone interview. "I told them exactly what happened. They were the first to hear it. There were certain details which they asked me not to talk about publicly, but I think in telling it everything should be disclosed. I can see no reason for anything being held back. The Air Force didn't want me to say that Zeeno told me the space people had no money. They did not want me to disclose the type and shape of the craft because they said that would indicate the Air Force was not doing its duty. I told them I could see no reason for that either. I *know* the Air Force believed it—I know it from the standpoint that they did a lot of checking down here in the area. They were here for quite some time after the incident...They didn't want me to divulge the saucer's means of communication or power. [Padrick was led to assume that the object was powered by light waves or magnetic rays]. Also, the man's name...they didn't want me to repeat that...because 'It didn't mean anything.' "

Reporters found that Sid Padrick was backed up by everyone who knew him. He was highly regarded as an honest man and was not a religious fanatic or UFO nut. Ironically, the hard-core UFO cultists rejected his story out of hand because of the unpalatable religious overtones. Everyone else, including the Air Force, took him very seriously.

Radio amateurs continue to receive strange messages from somewhere. Ham operators in certain areas have cautiously reported all kinds of manifestations, including the materialization of entities in their radio shacks. It is common for UFO contactees to hear alien voices delivering personal messages to them from their ordinary home receivers. A number of people even claim that images of the spacemen have appeared suddenly on their TV sets and addressed them directly. The rapid increase of such cases since 1965 suggests that a new game may be in the making. It sounds like a cheap science fiction plot, but a time may come when a general message to the human race may suddenly spurt from every receiver on earth in every language. Wouldn't that be a kick in the teeth!

During World War I very low frequencies (VLF) were briefly experimented with. These are very long radio waves which require a specially built receiver. In the last few decades VLF stations have quietly been constructed all over the world, although there are only a few commercial receivers on the market, and very few hams have VLF equipment. Most of that is of World War I vintage.

The U.S. Navy maintains several gigantic installations that cost billions of dollars and serve the announced purpose of communicating with our atomic submarines throughout the world's seas (VLF can penetrate underwater). To give some idea of their size, the largest commercial broadcasting station allowed puts out fifty thousand watts of power. The Voice of America has conventional stations that broadcast five hundred thousand watts. Yet the Soviet Union has a VLF station, in Odessa, that is pouring out *five million watts!* And the U.S. VLF station at Cutler, Maine, is putting out two million watts. There are now 150 VLF stations all over this planet, and aside from a few atomic submarines and a bevy of spies, there's no one to listen.

What are all these stations broadcasting? Well, station WWV transmits nothing but time signals...if anyone needs to set a watch. Teletypes are used by many stations exclusively. The teletype signal sounds somewhat musical, like bagpipes, over a loudspeaker. Voice transmission on the lower VLF channels is very difficult for a variety of reasons and not much of it is being done. Yet some amateurs with VLF equipment have reported picking up guttural, unintelligible voices at the very bottom of the scale around six kilohertz.

"All manner of strange (and often unexplained) radio sounds and signals mysteriously appear on VLF receivers," noted the *Radio-TV Experimenter,* April-May, 1967. (That issue gives details on how to build a VLF receiver for a few dollars.)

The government turned hundreds of square miles of Wisconsin into a massive VLF antenna, causing quite an uproar in that state. Every time the VLF transmitter is cranked up, telephones for miles around go amok with false rings and strange noises. In fact, many of the telephone problems currently plaguing the United States can probably be blamed on VLF experiments. These very long waves of electromagnetic energy can and do seriously affect equipment operating in the lower ranges of the spectrum.

Another culprit is the National Security Agency, the James Bondish organization that runs the CIA. We maintain a twenty-four-hour message service to our agents around the globe via VLF. These messages are broadcast in code on the higher VLF channels. A voice endlessly rattles off six-digit numbers. When the Cuban government arrested Humberto Carrillo Colon, an alleged CIA spy, in September 1969, they found a unique VLF transceiver in his possession. Cuban counterspies claimed they had been monitoring his transmissions for months and had broken the CIA code. Copies of Colon's alleged messages were released to the Havana newspapers and reprinted in

Communist propaganda organs in the United States. A number of oddities are buried in the dense text of these purported communiques with the CIA. In April 1969, Colon is supposed to have reported a conversation with a Cuban official: "On the way to the hotel he told me that I would be witness to something historical. THAT WITHIN SIX MONTHS THERE WOULD BE NO MORE MONEY." (Capitals were used in the published quote.) He allegedly saw "something strange, like a whale or large fish, that was no such thing, more like a mini-submarine or something like that") at Varadero. On October 8, 1968, during a visit to Holguin, he reported: "About 8:30 I saw a shooting star. First I saw a red light on the horizon very fast from right to left. I didn't give it any thought, but it was repeated twice more. I don't know what it was. I also saw a shooting star...I wasn't even drunk."

If the published reports are true—and of course, there is always room for doubt—then it would seem that CIA agents have been instructed to report anomalies and aerial phenomena.

In recent years voices calling off numbers on VLF channels have frequently been intercepted by conventional equipment when weather conditions were right. Tape recorders, sound movie projectors, TV sets, and even public address systems have been picking up these signals. For some reason, public address amplifiers in churches in England and the U.S. (such as the All Saints Roman Catholic Church in Portland, Oregon, and the St. Lawrence Church in Cambridge, England) have been especially prone to this type of interference. Listeners usually conclude they are hearing broadcasts of taxicab companies. Actually, taxi companies use a much higher frequency, and their signals are not likely to be picked up by low-frequency equipment. Television, incidentally, uses FM (frequency modulation) for sound, and it should be nearly impossible for a TV set to intercept any other signal.

At the other end of the radio spectrum on the ultrahigh frequencies (UHF) reserved exclusively for space satellites and manned spaceflight communications, there has also been a plague of anomalous radio signals. Back in November 1957, shortwave listeners everywhere were baffled by a strange tonal pattern that was broadcast next to the 20.005 frequency used by the two Russian satellites. Both the Soviet Union and the United States announced

emphatically that the signals were not related to the satellites. "It isn't clas-
sified," an FCC spokesman declared. "We just don't know what it is."

They never found out, either. The signals were much stronger than those
being broadcast by Sputniks I and II, they were worldwide, and they were
picked up by stations at times when the satellites were out of range on the
other side of the world.

During his fourth pass over Hawaii in MA-9 (Faith 7) on May 15, 1963,
astronaut Gordon Cooper's voice transmission was suddenly interrupted and
drowned out by "an unintelligible foreign language transmission" on the chan-
nel reserved for spaceflights—a frequency that few if any amateurs are equipped
to broadcast on. If the signal came from the ground, it had to come from
Hawaii (VHF and UHF are highly directional), but the FCC never arrested a
Hawaiian ham for the hoax. NASA recorded that transmission, a voice grunt-
ing and speaking rapidly in a language that has never been identified.

Later space shots have been repeatedly troubled by these anomalous
transmissions. The broadcasts from our astronauts circling the moon in 1968
and 1969 were often interrupted by strange noises. Anyone listening to those
NASA transmissions closely heard things like Indian war whoops and strange
music. Because the space channels are highly directional, these odd inser-
tions *had to come from space* or from specially equipped planes flying
directly over the directional dish antennae used to pick up the astronaut's
transmissions. NASA has been uneasily silent about its investigations into
these problems.

All of the American astronauts and Soviet cosmonauts have seen and
photographed unusual lights and objects in space. The annual report of the
Colorado University UFO study devotes a full chapter to the unexplained
astronaut sightings.

The late Frank Edwards, a famous radio newsman and author of flying
saucer books, made much of the weird radio signals that had been received
in Uppsala, Sweden, in 1961 (the same area where the ghost-flier broadcasts
had been received in 1934). A group of young radio enthusiasts had built
tracking equipment and receivers that could pick up the high frequencies
employed by the American and Soviet space programs. As soon as they had

their equipment in operation, they picked up an extended (it lasted seven days and nights) series of broadcasts, apparently from orbiting manned space vehicles. These were in Russian and were taped and translated. A hapless pair of cosmonauts was presumably lost in space. They discussed the critical situation they were in and wearily concluded, "The world will never know about it anyway…"

They were wrong. Other amateur tracking stations in Italy and Alaska were also tuned in, according to Edwards.

Edwards' conclusion was that the Russians sent two cosmonauts into space, and they had been killed. There is one problem: The Soviet space program was nowhere nearly advanced enough for such an effort in 1961. Yuri Gagarin had made his historic orbital flight—the world's first—only one month before the signals were received. The next manned flight would require months of preparation. The Soviets could not and would not have attempted a twin mission at that point in their program. It is much more probable that the radio transmissions were the work of our mysterious radio hoaxsters.

We can offer many other examples of complicated and seemingly pointless radio hoaxes. A frantic distress signal swept the Pacific early in 1968 and was received by marine radio stations and ships at sea. The signals were triangulated and the exact position of a purportedly distressed freighter was determined. Following the law of the sea, several ships in the vicinity changed their courses and rushed to the aid of the sinking vessel.

There was one slight hitch. The freighter in question was safely docked in the harbor at Calcutta, India, and the would-be rescuers found nothing but empty ocean.

A few months later the atomic submarine *Scorpion* vanished in the Atlantic in the section popularly known as the Bermuda Triangle. Once again mysterious radio signals were received by several ships and naval stations and were triangulated, pinpointing the exact position. These signals were broadcast on the VLF frequency reserved for atomic submarines and used the secret code names employed by the Navy. Planes and rescue vessels rushed to the spot and found nothing. In December 1968, the Navy issued a statement announcing that the *Scorpion* had finally been located hundreds of miles away from the spot where the signals had presumably originated. The signals were denounced as a hoax.

What kind of hoax? Did some practical joker load some rare VLF equipment into a small boat after somehow stealing a copy of the Navy's secret code book? Did he then sail out into the middle of the Atlantic, broadcast his false signals, and then somehow sail back, managing to elude the planes and rescue ships on the way?

Anomalous radio broadcasts also played a baffling role in the assassinations. Four minutes after Kennedy was shot in Dallas, Texas, in 1963, someone was broadcasting on the police bands in Dallas, offering a description of Lee Harvey Oswald. This was long before the police had even heard of Oswald or had any reason to think he might have been implicated in the assassination. None of the regular police dispatchers had broadcast that alarm. Who did? The question remains unanswered.

Immediately after the Rev. Martin Luther King was shot in Memphis, Tennessee, in April 1968, a phony broadcast on the police band sent all the police rushing to the wrong side of town, while the alleged killer went off in the other direction unhindered.

Our radio pranksters are a fact, not a myth. They operate in all languages and are obviously equipped with rare, specialized transmitters so powerful they can drown out all conventional signals. Their enterprises are usually pointless, sometimes harmful, never explainable. It must be a very expensive operation...*if* it is purely terrestrial. But many of these incidents smack of the mischievous work of our ultraterrestrials.

Our phantom broadcasters have also zeroed in on supersophisticated scientific equipment. At 4:00 A.M. on the morning of April 8, 1960, the great dish antenna of the radio telescope at Green Bank, West Virginia, swept across the skies and focused upon the predetermined target: Epsilon Eridani and Tau Ceti. This was Project Ozma, the search for intelligent signals from outer space, headed by Dr. Otto Struve and Dr. Frank Drake. They tuned their equipment to 1420.4 megacycles (they had calculated that communication over vast stellar distances would be most feasible at this wavelength—the frequency of hydrogen). Eureka! Even before they could switch on their loudspeakers a powerful signal blasted in, "knocking the needles off the dials," as Drake put it. They received a very strong series of pulses, about eight per second, so uniform that they *had* to come from an intelligent source.

After recovering from their initial excitement, the scientists rechecked every part of their equipment but could find nothing wrong. The signals lasted for about five minutes and then stopped abruptly. Later the Naval Research Laboratory revealed that its staff had been listening to these same signals for the past six months.

Two weeks later the men at Green Bank tuned into the signals again. This time they carefully moved their antenna away from the two stars as they listened, and they found the signals continued to come in loud and clear. This proved that the transmissions were not coming from a star but were very probably of local, terrestrial origin from some unknown but amazingly powerful transmitter.

Rumors that secret radar experiments were responsible for the signals proved unfounded. Radar does not use that wavelength, does not pulse eight times per second, and could not affect the highly directional radio telescope.

A trio of Soviet scientists, Gennady E. Sholomitsky, Nikolai S. Kardashev, and I.S.Shklovskii, won worldwide headlines in 1965 when they announced that they had received radio signals from beacons of some supercivilization in space. Later other radio astronomers discovered that these signals were coming from fantastically huge stars labeled quasars, the furthest out of all known objects in the universe. The signals are apparently natural radio propagation. The Russians later retracted their theories about the supercivilization, causing the UFO buffs to howl "Coverup!" once more.

In 1967, Dr. Drake and other scientists working at the Arecibo, Puerto Rico, radio-telescope installation detected waves of hissing and static coming from four different points. Experimentation revealed numerous other invisible sources of radio waves in space and these objects have been tagged pulsars. The current theory is that pulsars are the hard-core remnants of a supernova that has collapsed inwardly and is made up of densely packed neutrons. So far it seems that the magnetic fields of the pulsars are one trillion times greater than the earth's. The sky may be filled with these things, and if any should ever happen to wander into our solar system, things could become very uncomfortable on this planet.

Sadly, the United States lags far behind in radio-telescope research. Germany, Britain, Holland, Australia, and even Argentina and Israel are building bigger and better instruments to probe into these new mysteries.

Meanwhile mankind is unwittingly overloading or overcharging the earth's atmosphere with all kinds of magnetic and radio waves. As the man-made electromagnetic field increases, it clashes with the natural magnetism of the earth. The result is that apparatus dependent on small magnetic fields (such as generators, computers, and tape recorders) is now being thrown askew by these larger blankets of incompatible electromagnetism.

Nikola Tesla calculated that the earth's natural fields lie at a frequency of about 150 kilocycles. Perhaps when there is an interchange between the earth's fields and the rays or fields coming in from stellar sources such as pulsars, an overcharge develops in some areas, inducing power failures and malfunctions of electronic equipment. One of the few really secure facts in ufology is that there have been hundreds of power failures simultaneous with the appearance of unidentified flying objects. The popular notion that UFOs cause power failures could be erroneous. It is possible that the appearance of UFOs and the accompanying power failures could in some cases be the result of this cosmic energy exchange.

During the great Northeastern Blackout of 1965 several local power companies *completely independent of the affected main power grid* also failed. Interestingly, while normal AM radio frequencies continued to operate that night, short wave and VLF transmission and reception in the affected regions were hopelessly jammed with static. This alone indicates that an extraordinary electromagnetic condition existed. Following the big blackout, New York's Con Edison power company quietly installed expensive magnetic shielding devices around key equipment and new, heavily shielded cables were introduced in sensitive areas. After 1965 Bell Telephone Company began switching from overhead lines to more expensive, heavily shielded cables buried under the ground.

In the summer of 1970 all the electronic gear in the videotape studios of Waddell & Reed, Inc., in Kansas City, Missouri, went haywire.

"Something made our equipment completely sensitive to everything around us," the manager of the studio, Mrs. Kevin Eisenbrandt, told the *Kansas City Star* (August 5, 1970). The nearby Commerce Bank experienced similar problems with their computers and electronic gear at the same time. Experts called in to investigate were baffled.

In far-off Noebbet, Denmark, a sawmill closed down in October 1970, economically ruined "by mysterious forces that have blown out fuses by the thousands, bulbs by the hundreds, and electric motors by the dozen." Hans Nielsen, the owner, told reporters that the disturbances began eighteen months earlier. Scientists and technicians measured twenty-nine thousand "lightning-like electrical discharges in mill installations in one day." The bursts occurred even when all electricity to the mill was cut off.

Incidents such as these are on the increase. Electromagnetic pollution is becoming a serious worldwide problem. Another more grisly aspect of the phenomenon, death by lightning, is also on the rise. A worldwide wave of lightning deaths took place in August and September 1970. In a number of cases the fatal lightning bolts lashed out of a clear, cloudless sky.

Satellites whizzing around the earth have detected a powerful beam of VLF energy being projected intermittently from a specific area of empty ocean near Antarctica. This has inspired scientific speculation that the earth may be broadcasting natural radio waves into space on the same order of the waves coming from Jupiter and Venus. A few years ago newspapers carried a puzzling report from Greenland, describing how a group of scientists there had discovered a massive object buried deep in the ice. It supposedly broadcast a strange radio signal at regular intervals. This odd report was never verified, and nothing further was ever published about it.

One of the persistent UFO rumors of the early 1950s claimed that an unnamed scientist in Washington had in his possession a tiny box that had been extracted from a "crashed flying saucer in New Mexico." According to the rumor, the box emitted a loud beep every fifteen minutes and no one could figure out what it was made of or how it worked.

Radio itself is supposed to have been one of the secrets of the ancient mystical societies: a closely guarded means of communication between members. A form of primitive crystal sets was allegedly used by the brothers of the Rosenkreuz (Rosy Cross—the Rosicrucians) centuries ago. It is even possible—there is no way of knowing for sure—that the mysterious plates and amulets used by ancient priests may have been crystal sets of some sort, tuned to some secret mountain transmitter.

We do know that the atmosphere of our haunted planet is overloaded with electrical energy today, ranging from man-made radio signals on every frequency to mysterious, patterned signals from some unknown source. While our scientists have been tuning their multi-million-dollar equipment into remote hisses and squeaks from distant stars, hundreds, if not thousands, of ham radio operators and teenagers with homemade coils and condensers have been listening with awe to the wild, unidentifiable, and obviously intelligent signals radiating from and around our own planet. These signals exist. They existed from the moment Tesla first tuned into them accidentally. If the present trend continues, more and more people will be hearing these strange voices and signals from their radios and TV sets in the future. We live in a world ruled by electromagnetism, and there is every indication that someone—the earth's phantom inhabitants—learned to utilize these forces long ago. In time we may learn to separate the natural static and the CIA codes from the truly enigmatic waves that are flowing all around us.

Chapter Fifteen

Where Is Everybody Going?

STRANGE THINGS HAPPEN on the twenty-fourth of the month. People vanish. On October 24, 1593, a Spanish soldier standing guard in Manila in the Philippines suddenly disappeared. Twenty-four hours later he found himself in Mexico City, some nine thousand miles from Manila, without any idea how he had managed to travel so far so fast. We could dismiss the seemingly factual historic account of this case if it weren't for the disturbing fact that such things continue to happen on a regular basis.

On October 24, 1967, Bruce Burkan, nineteen, found himself sitting in a bus terminal in Newark, dressed in a cheap, ill-fitting suit with exactly seven cents in his pocket. He didn't have the foggiest notion what he was doing there, nor could he remember anything that had happened during the previous two months. On August 22, 1967, Burkan and his girlfriend went to a beach at Ashbury Park, New Jersey. He left her later to go and put a coin in a parking meter. He was wearing nothing but a bathing suit. When he failed to return, his friend went looking for him. She found his locked car where he had parked it.

Burkan's family held a well publicized search for him, but not a single clue turned up. Finally they conducted a funeral service in his memory, giving him up for dead. After his reappearance on October 24 the young man told reporters, "There's one thing that really bothers me. I have fiery red hair. Where was I that despite all the publicity no one recognized me?"

On August 15, 1967, seven days before Burkan's still unexplained disappearance, a thirty-seven-year-old research scientist named Paul T. Mac-Gregor left his office at the Polaroid Corporation in Boston, Massachusetts, and started out for Camp Kirby to join his vacationing family. He never got there. One month later he walked into a police station in Buffalo, New York, and told them he didn't know who he was. His identity was traced through the labels of his clothes and the inscription on his wedding ring. Doctors at the Meyer Memorial Hospital examined him and said they were convinced that he was suffering from amnesia.

Who or what had met him on that Massachusetts highway that night and caused his mind to shut off the past?

Despite all the movie and soap opera plots that have revolved around amnesia, a simple blow on the head rarely induces the condition. The traditional medical explanation is that an overwhelming emotional trauma is the cause of most amnesia. A man murders his wife in a fit of rage, and then his mind wipes out his entire memory. A child sees his dog run over by a car and erases the painful memory by blotting out that entire period of his childhood. Skilled psychiatrists can spot this form of amnesia and cope with it. But most of the amnesia cases induced by paranormal happenings, such as encounters with fairies or flying saucers, are not so easily diagnosed and dealt with. The nature of the trauma is never fully determined.

Every July there is a sudden rash of new amnesia cases in the national press, coinciding with the traditional July peak of UFO sightings. Thousands of people who have been exposed to psychic phenomena and UFO manifestations have suffered lacunal amnesia; that is, they find they are unable to remember a short period of time before, during, or after their experiences. Others appear suddenly in different parts of the world, sometimes knowing who they are but baffled that they are suddenly so far from home. A Londoner suddenly finds himself in South Africa. A girl from Cleveland awakens to discover she is in Australia. An unemployed Swedish milkman suddenly finds himself on a golf course on a remote island resort for the very rich.

A woman in Allentown, Pennsylvania, soberly related this strange story: she said she and her husband maintained a small summer cottage in the Pocono Mountains, a mere thirty-minute drive from their home. One Saturday morning in July 1966, the young couple got into their car and started out for the cottage. As they drove along the Pennsylvania Turnpike, which seemed strangely devoid of traffic that day, they saw a large circular object in the sky ahead of them. It looked as if it was going to land directly on the turnpike, she said. Her husband, mildly alarmed, pulled over to the edge of the road and stopped. They watched as the object, a shiny metallic thing with large black spots or windows, flew very low ever their car. Then it was suddenly gone. Her husband started the car again and they drove on to their cottage. It was not until after they arrived at their destination that they looked at their watches. It was 1:30 P.M. They had started out at 9:30 A.M. For some reason that neither of them could understand, it took them four hours to make a drive that normally took thirty minutes!

On a warm night early in August 1966, a Philadelphia policeman named Chester Archey, Jr., set out on a routine patrol in North Philadelphia. He drove instead through that door into the unknown. Archey, a veteran of fifteen years on the force, suddenly found himself in Pennsauken, New Jersey, where he became involved in a minor accident as he drove around in confusion. "I don't have any idea how I got there," Archey protested at a police hearing later. "I don't even know where Pennsauken is!"

In occult and UFO lore there are hundreds of reports of this phenomenon. It also seems to work in reverse. Witnesses claim that they drove or even walked incredible distances—sometimes hundreds of miles—in incredibly short periods of time. It is as if they crossed over into another dimension where time and space have a different relationship.

There is also a peculiar cloud phenomenon connected with some of these teleportations, or transferences. According to the newspaper *Diario de Córdoba*, a well-known Argentine businessman suffered a strange distortion of time and space in 1959. He reportedly got into his brand-new car one morning in the city of Bahia Blanca, Argentina, and started to drive away from his hotel when a strange cloud seemed to envelop his vehicle. The next thing he knew he was *standing* alone on a deserted spot in the countryside. He hailed a passing truck and asked the driver to take him to Bahia Blanca. Looking at him as if he were some kind of maniac, the driver explained that they were in Salta. Bahia Blanca was over a thousand kilometers away! He drove the befuddled businessman to the nearest police station, and they called the police in Bahia Blanca. The police later called back and confirmed that the businessman's car was still outside the hotel with its engine running. Strangest of all, only a few minutes had elapsed from the time the man had first climbed into the car—yet he had somehow been transported over a thousand kilometers.

Bahia Blanca is a busy Window area and has been the site of many strange psychic and UFO reports in recent years. In May 1968, Dr. Gerardo Vidal and his wife said they were driving outside the city when their auto was caught up in a dense fog and they lost consciousness. They came to on a strange road. Their watches had stopped and the surface of their car was badly scorched. They soon learned that forty-eight hours had passed, and they were now in *Mexico,* many thousands of miles north of Bahia Blanca!

On March 4, 1964, a leading Japanese newspaper, *Mainichi*, carried an unbelievable story about an automobile disappearing in full view of a crowded highway. The reporting witnesses were three officials of the Fuji Bank on their way to the golf course at Ryugazaki. As they drove outside of Kana-machi, they said they saw a black car ahead of them going in the same direction. Aside from the driver, they could see an elderly man in the back seat reading a newspaper.

"Suddenly a puff of something gaseous, like white smoke or vapor, gushed from somewhere around the black car, and when this cloud dispersed (a matter of not more than five seconds), the black car had vanished," the newspaper account said.

The trio of witnesses were so shaken by the incident that they stopped and reported it to the police, and so another inexplicable oddity was added to our bulging files. Could that car in Japan have been taken by the same unknown force that transported the Argentine businessman a thousand kilometers? Could the same force have been at work when British Wing Commander J. Baldwin flew into a cloud and *never came out again* during the Korean War? Other pilots in his formation scoured the area but could find no trace of their commander or his plane. Was it the same kind of cloud that literally devoured a whole regiment of British soldiers near Sulva Bay, Turkey, in 1915? An entrenched group of men later signed affidavits swearing they had watched the One-Fourth Norfolk Regiment march into a peculiar brown cloud that hugged the ground in their path and that none of them reappeared on the other side. After a few moments the cloud rose up and flew away, the witnesses reported, joining a group of similar clouds, which then sailed off against the wind. No one from that regiment was ever seen again. Eight hundred men gone—or taken—from the face of the earth!

On August 4, 1968, Graciela del Lourdes Cimenez, eleven, was playing outside her home in Córdoba, Argentina, when she too was caught up in one of these mysterious clouds.

"I wanted to go back indoors and watch TV," she told reporters from the newspaper *Córdoba,* "and then just as I was about to turn around...a white cloud, like mist, appeared on the front path. It gradually came towards where I was, and then I could no longer see the other houses, and I couldn't move or call out to Mummy...And after that...I don't know anything more...until I found myself on a square where there were lots of people and lots of little boys..."

She knocked at a nearby house, and the residents turned her over to the police. How had she traveled from a Córdoba suburb to the Plaza Espania in the heart of the city? Mr. Cordon Creighton, a retired British consular officer, collected the reports and translated them for *Flying Saucer Review*, September-October, 1970. He reported that the child suffered fits of weeping and cold chills following the incident.

There are periodic waves of disappearances that create brief sensations in the newspapers and are quickly forgotten. No one ever manages to find out where these people have gone. In 1912 five men, all unrelated, disappeared unaccountably in a single week in Buffalo, New York. Montreal, Canada, had a wave of missing persons in July 1883, and again in July 1892.

Children vanish more frequently than any other group. We're not talking about ordinary runaways. In August 1869, thirteen children vanished in Cork, Ireland. No sign of kidnapping or foul play. That same month there was a wave of disappearing children in Brussels, Belgium. Another group of youngsters melted away in Belfast in August 1895. And again in August 1920, eight girls (all under twelve years of age) disappeared forever in Belfast.

The latter part of the nineteenth century produced several classic disappearances. On Thursday, September 23, 1880, a farmer named David Lang took a few steps into an open field near Gallatin, Tennessee, and vanished instantaneously in front of several witnesses, including Judge August Peck. Where did he go? A long and thorough search of the field never produced an answer. Five years later on Thursday, April 23, 1885, another farmer named Isaac Martin walked into a field near Salem, Virginia, and like David Lang, dissolved into nothingness.

Christmas Eve (a twenty-fourth, naturally), 1889, an eleven-year-old boy named Oliver Larch joined the legion of the missing when he went outside his home near South Bend, Indiana, to get a pail of water. His family heard him cry out, "Help! Help! They've got me!" His footprints led fifty feet away in the fresh snow and then stopped. His bucket lay a few feet beyond that point. There were no other marks of any kind. It was as if Oliver Larch had been scooped into the sky off the face of the earth.

This type of sudden, inexplicable disappearance still takes place. In the summer of 1969 a seven-year-old boy named Dennis Martin was whisked away in Great Smoky Mountains National Park in Tennessee. One second he was walking along with his father and other relatives, the next second he was gone. Every stone and crevice was searched. A massive hunt was launched with more than fourteen hundred people looking under every bush. The boy was never found.

Children began to disappear in the city of Villa Velha, Brazil, early in December 1969, according to Brazilian correspondent Eduardo Keffel of the German magazine *Die Bunte Illustriette*, March 24, 1970. Within a few weeks a minor mystery had exploded into a frightening epidemic. Scores of youngsters, all between the ages of nine and fifteen and all from poor families (ruling out any ransom motive), vanished without a trace. The police in the state of Espirito Santo rallied their forces and began a massive search for a sinister kidnapping ring. But they had no leads. The disappearances seemed random, were not ordinary runaways, and none of the children knew each other or shared a common school.

Then in February 1970, four of the missing youngsters reappeared separately. Two were stumbling about the streets blindly, suffering from amnesia. The other pair were able to remember fragments of their adventure, but their stories were as bizarre as a James Bond tale. They had been stopped on the street, they said, and offered a ride in a large American-style limousine (quite a treat to a poor Brazilian youngster). Once they were in the car, they were given a cigarette (apparently drugged) and they lapsed into unconsciousness. One returnee recalled that he awoke in a small hut, tied hand and foot, when a stranger entered, freed him, and told him how to find the nearest police station. An eleven-year-old girl identified as Vani said her kidnapper was a woman named Laura. Laura fed her sweets and then took her to a field where an airplane was waiting. Vani began to scream and fuss, and surprisingly Laura gave her some money and returned her to her village.*

Most of the Brazilian victims were boys, although a few girls were included. Once the kidnapping wave received publicity, a number of youths had narrow escapes, fleeing the big cars and their mysterious occupants when they were offered a lift. Local police never caught up with these cars and speculated they were dealing with some kind of slavery ring.

Actually, children have been disappearing in large numbers for centuries all over the world, and most of these cases have remained unsolved. In the Middle Ages, it was popularly believed that fairies and leprechauns frequently stole children away. The Indians of North and South America also have many myths and stories about children being kidnapped by the little people. The notion that parahumans kidnap children is deeply entrenched in every culture. In more recent times Gypsies have often been accused of kidnapping.

---

*Jessup discussed the case of the teleported Spanish soldier mentioned at the opening of this chapter in his book, *The Case for the UFO*. Among the annotations in the later Varo edition there was a pointed description of how the soldier had made so much trouble that they decided to let him go.

The celebrated Pied Piper of Hameln, Germany, is more than just a charming children's story. A stranger actually did appear in Hameln in the Middle Ages, and he lured away 150 children never seen again. The event is still commemorated with an annual festival in Hameln.

In A.D. 1212 a teenage boy in France, Stephen of Cloyes, began to hear voices that inspired him to collect together fifty thousand children for the pathetic Children's Crusade. They marched to do battle with the infidels and disappeared *en masse*. The popular explanation is that they were all seized by slavers.

One of the first colonies to be established in the New World—the Roanoke Island colony begun in 1585 off the coast of what is now North Carolina—disappeared magically. Virginia Dare, the first child of European descent to be born on this continent, was among the missing. The local Indians were not hostile and were as baffled by the vanishing colony as the explorers who came searching for it.

Another entire village, a remote Eskimo settlement in northern Canada, lost its entire population sometime in August,1930. The Northwest Mounted Police found the village abandoned, but its thirty inhabitants had left behind their food, clothing, kayaks, rifles, and dogs. Since no Eskimo is likely to travel very far without his precious rifle or his dog, the police were baffled. A two-week investigation of the area failed to yield any clues. Strangest of all, a grave on the edge of the village had been opened, and the body was gone. Grave robbing is an unspeakable crime among the Eskimos, and it is very unlikely that they dug up the body and fled the village, leaving behind their weapons, tools, food, and their dogs.

At the other end of the world in Antarctica an American scientist vanished without a trace on May 7, 1965. He was Carl Robert Disch, twenty-six, and he was assigned to the Byrd Station, operating equipment to investigate VLF radio noises for the National Bureau of Standards. He set out to walk from his hut to the main station a short distance away, following a hand line that was strung as a guide for the path between the two points. When he failed to appear after forty-five minutes, the other scientists went out searching for him in tracked vehicles.

"If Disch had fallen and was lying in the snow," Ron Sefton, the leader of the Byrd Station explained to William J. Perkinson of the *Baltimore Sun,* "the huskies would have seen him long before the searchers did. Similarly, if he had fallen and was covered by drifting snow, the dogs would have sighted the mound and rushed out to investigate it. That's the way huskies are."

The search went on for three days and covered a thirty-five-mile area around the hut. Disch's own dog, a husky called Gus, disappeared shortly afterwards. Some of the searchers claimed they saw mysterious lights and heard engine noises in the distance. Antarctica is, of course, uninhabited except for a handful of international scientists who work very closely with one another.

Airplanes, ships and submarines have also disappeared by the hundreds. In quite a few cases the missing ships or planes were later found, mysteriously abandoned by their crews. One of the first and most celebrated of these incidents took place on July 24, 1924, when Lt. W. T. Day and Pilot Officer D. R. Stewart went off in a single-engined biplane for a routine patrol over the Arab desert. A search party found their plane the next day, parked on the desert and completely intact, in excellent working order. There was gasoline in the tank, and no sign of trouble or violence. The footprints of the two men were clearly visible in the sand. They had taken a few steps away from the plane—and then the footprints ended abruptly. Like young Oliver Larch, they had taken a stroll into thin air.

An Italian ufologist, Alberto Fenoglio, reported rumors of a similar disappearance in the Soviet Union in 1961. A small mail plane was reported missing but was quickly located in perfect shape near the remote town of Tobolsk, Siberia. "Everything on board—engine, radio, mailbags, etc.—was in perfect order," Fenoglio stated. "The tank contained fuel for two hours of flight. The four passengers had vanished without a trace. A distance of about three hundred feet from the aircraft there was a huge, clearly defined circle on which the grass was all scorched and the earth depressed."

Over fifty pilots and men of the United States Air Force have lost their lives or disappeared suddenly while pursuing unidentified flying objects. Their deaths have been officially documented. Their names and the peculiar circumstances surrounding these tragedies have been released to a bewildered and sometimes disbelieving press and public. Some of these incidents involved aerial collisions with *invisible* objects.

On June 11, 1938, the *Chicago Daily News* described the crash of a U.S. Army bomber outside of Delaware, Illinois. Nine men were killed after what one ground witness described as a "sudden crash in midair." Crash with what? No one knows.

Three more pilots died on June 8, 1951, when four jets crashed simultaneously near Richmond, Indiana. Another four jets came to a strange end near Lawrenceville, Georgia, on December 3, 1953. The tower operators at the Dobbins Air Base heard one of the pilots exclaim, "We can't miss it!" Moments later all four planes came diving out of the clouds in flames.

After a thorough study of the debris of a jetliner which crashed outside Calcutta on May 2, 1953, the British Ministry of Civil Aviation announced that it had "collided with a fairly heavy body." Witnesses said that there was no other plane near the doomed airliner when it "seemed to stop short in midair" and crashed.

A B-47 smacked into something solid in October 1955, and only one man survived. He was quoted in the newspaper accounts as saying that the plane was "struck in midair," and the jolt was so terrific he thought they had struck the ground. The crash took place near Lovington, New Mexico, and authorities said there were no other planes in the vicinity. One ground witness did claim, however, that a ball of fire appeared near the plane just before the crash. A couple of weeks later, another B-47 met with an identical fate in Texas. Witnesses said they saw "a ball of fire with sparks shooting out of it" just before the plane went down.

Are there invisible things haunting our airways, endangering planes, pilots, and passengers?

Ufologist Jerome Clark uncovered an extraordinary item from an old 1939 newspaper. "On a day in late summer, 1939, a military transport left the Marine Naval Air Station in San Diego, California, for a routine flight to Honolulu," Clark wrote in *Flying Saucer Review*. "About three hours afterwards several urgent distress signals sounded from the plane and then silence.

Later the craft came limping back to execute an emergency landing. When Air Station personnel entered the plane, they found every man of the crew, including the copilot who had lived long enough to pilot the craft back to its base, dead of unknown causes.

> Each of the bodies carried large, gaping wounds, and the outside of the ship was similarly marked. Air Station men who touched parts of the craft came down with a mysterious skin infection.
>
> One of the most puzzling aspects of the whole affair was that the .45 automatics carried by the pilot and copilot as service pieces had been emptied, and the shells lay on the floor. A smell of rotten eggs pervaded the atmosphere inside the plane…Mysterious skin infections and rotten egg odors [hydrogen sulfide] are phenomena familiar to all UFO researchers. It would seem that the transport was attacked—apparently without provocation—by some sort of strange aerial intruder.

Air Force records show that one of the first cases of an electromagnetic effect took place over Iwo Jima on August 28, 1945, when a C-46's engines failed as three UFOs maneuvered around it. In those days military men called UFOs *Foo Fighters*. The Foo Fighters baffled both Allied and Axis pilots over Germany and Japan in the final days of the war. Bomber crews were also reporting constant appearances of little green men who invaded their planes and caused all kinds of mischief. The press labeled them Gremlins and the popular conclusion was that the crews were merely hallucinating because of the high altitude and thin atmosphere. Since then there have been thousands of little green men reports from all over the world. They are now an integral part of the flying saucer lore.

People in Florida were also watching aircraft in the fall of 1945, the common assumption being that the objects were some kind of new secret weapon. Then on December 5, 1945, one of the most famous disappearances in history occurred. Five TBM Avenger torpedo bombers took off from Fort Lauderdale Naval Air Station on a routine training mission. Fourteen men were aboard. Although the weather was perfect, the flight soon ran into some kind of trouble. Radio contact with the base ended abruptly.

A Martin Mariner flying boat carrying a crew of thirteen was sent up to find the missing Flight 19. Twenty minutes after it took off radio communications with it also ended abruptly.

Altogether, twenty-seven men and six planes completely disappeared a few miles off the Florida coast that afternoon An extensive search by land, sea, and air was conducted for weeks afterwards. It was one of the biggest searches in history, and it failed to turn up a single piece of debris… not even an oil slick.

The disappearance of Flight 19 and the rescue plane sparked the official beginning of the Bermuda Triangle mystery. In the more than fifty years since, in excess of thirty planes have vanished in the lozenge-shaped area southwest of Bermuda, carrying with them a total of some three hundred people. A number of ships, together with their entire crews, have also melted away there forever. Such incidents can be traced back as far as 1846. Ivan Sanderson, who made a study of this phenomenon, believed there are at least six of these vile vortices, as he calls them, spaced evenly around the world. The Devil's Sea off the coast of Japan, for example, has swallowed up so many ships that fisherman carefully sail around it.

The Navy took the disappearance of Flight 19 very seriously. In January 1946, a group of Naval Intelligence officers were ordered by President Truman to form an investigative body called the Central Intelligence Group. This was the forerunner to the CIA. In the spring of 1946 the CIG participated in a series of secret hearings in Washington. The wives and relatives of the missing men were flown to Washington to attend the meetings. Since then most of these people have refused to discuss the subject at all. But one mother of a missing man did confide to researcher Art Ford, the famous disk jockey who made a hobby of investigating the Flight 19 case, that she believed her son was still alive "somewhere…maybe in space."

During 1965–66, the National Bureau of Standards mounted special microphones and instruments along the coastline facing the Bermuda Triangle to try to pick up sounds that might lie above the range of human hearing. They succeeded in recording odd whispering sounds of unknown origin. The Navy quietly conducted a new search of the Triangle in 1967, spending over five million dollars to search the ocean floors with special research submarines and devices. As usual, they failed to find any trace of the missing planes and ships. and were unable to come up with any new explanation for the mystery.

Sanderson's cautious theory about the vile vortices, as expounded in his book, *Invisible Residents*, is that these areas are plagued with magnetic and gravitational anomalies. Maybe the planes fell up!

In the summer of 1970, a giant Soviet cargo plane carrying supplies to earthquake-stricken Peru disappeared south of Greenland. Planes from several countries searched the area for days and failed to find a trace of it. That September three adventurers set out in a balloon from New York, hoping to cross the Atlantic. They too vanished and repeated searches could not locate their supposedly unsinkable gondola.

Everyone has heard of the *Marie Celeste*, the ship found floating crewless in the Atlantic in 1872. There have been scores of similar finds. Usually such ships are completely intact, often with food cooking on the stoves and the galley tables set for dinner. The crews and passengers simply abandon ship, leaving all their personal effects behind. Five such ships were found adrift in the Bermuda Triangle area during June-July 1969.

In the spring of 1969, a British sailor named John Fairfax was crossing the Atlantic alone when he reportedly observed two brilliant lights on the horizon. They separated and flew higher into the sky. As he watched, fascinated, he claims he entered a motionless, trancelike state. "It was more than just seeing them," he related afterwards. "It was this force. It was as though they were saying to me: 'Do you want to come with us?' And I was fighting it and saying back: 'No, no, no!' It was like telepathy, like being hypnotized."

After the objects swooped away, Fairfax realized for the first time that the cigarette he was holding had burned his fingers.

In January 1970, another ship drifted ashore at the island of Trinidad. It was the *Sta Filomena* and had accommodations for seven persons. There was no one on board.

A C-46 loaded with five tons of meat disappeared over the Caribbean in April 1970. The usual fruitless search was conducted.

Submarines too have shown a tendency to vanish in tightly spaced waves or cycles. Back in 1939 before World War II got under way, four subs vanished in four months. They belonged to Japan, the United States, Great Britain, and France. During the week of January 21, 1968, both a French and Israeli submarine disappeared without a trace in the placid Mediterranean. They were hundreds of miles apart when they performed a disappearing act almost simultaneously. Searching parties reported unidentified flying objects in the area, and one group of would-be rescuers detected a metal object and thought they had found one of the missing craft. But the object scooted away and was never explained. Since then four more subs belonging to the United States, England, and France have vanished. The French *Eurydice* was swallowed up on Wednesday, March 4, 1970, in the Mediterranean. Somebody seems to be collecting submarines.

People, planes, ships, submarines, and even automobiles are constantly disappearing suddenly and inexplicably all over this haunted planet of ours. Naturally, these mysteries have attracted the flying saucer researchers, and two ufologists apparently joined the missing voluntarily on November 11, 1953. Wilbur J. Wilkinson held a responsible position with the Hoffman Radio Corporation in Los Angeles and according to his wife, "had tape recordings of conversations with men from other planets who landed here in saucers." The den in his home was lined with UFO photographs and weird symbols and formulations, supposedly passed along by little men from the planet Maser who were preparing to invade earth. Wilkinson's partner, Karl Hunrath, claimed to have information about landed saucers and talked his friend into renting an airplane so they could try to find it. They took off from the Gardena, California, airport with a three-hour supply of gasoline. That was the last anyone saw of them. A widespread search failed to turn up either the plane or the two men.

At least one eyewitness claims to have seen a UFO seize a plane in midair and carry it off. Eugene Metcalfe of Paris, Illinois, has signed a notarized affidavit avowing that on Wednesday, March 9, 1955, he was watching a jet fighter shoot across the sky when suddenly a gigantic object "shaped like a call bell" descended over it. This object, Metcalfe said, literally swallowed up the fast-moving jet "as easy as a hawk would a chicken" and then disappeared upward with its prey. A fighter and its pilot were reported missing in the region that day.

In earlier times the ultraterrestrials established religions among men that, while they seemed benevolent, introduced the practice of making human sacrifices to the gods. This barbaric sacrificial rite was common throughout Europe, Asia, the Pacific, and South America for thousands of years. Only the finest specimens of the tribe were accepted for sacrifice—beautiful young virgins and muscular young men. In most cultures the victims volunteered. It was in fact a very high honor. They were feted before they were led to a high holy place or the top of a pyramid. In some cultures they were taken to a sacred island and left there. They were always gone the next month or year when the tribe returned with new sacrificial victims.

Physical sacrifice continued into biblical times and persisted in some cultures until only a few centuries ago. The brutal inquisitions of the Middle Ages claimed more millions of victims and included mass disappearances of people who were presumably hauled off to some dungeon never to be seen again. Robed and hooded men pounded on doors in the middle of the night and dragged away whole families.

The record shows that the ultraterrestrials have a need for physical human beings. Once they were quite open in demanding specimens to serve that need. Times have changed though, and their methods are more subtle. Thousands of people disappear annually without a trace (not counting the hundreds of thousands who are fleeing the law, creditors, and spouses). They once exploited the human race in the guise of benevolent gods living on hilltops; they now exploit us through the modern myth of extraterrestrial visitors from distant stars.

Perhaps the planet earth is nothing more than a gigantic farm. We unfortunately are the crop.

Chapter Sixteen

The Revolution of the Mind

THE NEW MAN IS LIVING amongst us now! He is here!" Adolf Hitler declared. "I have seen the new man. He is intrepid and cruel. I was afraid of him."

Hitler's Germany was a phenomenon that will be studied by scholars for centuries to come. This mad genius created the ultimate secret society. He exhumed all the ancient symbols—the swastika was an old Oriental symbol—and gathered around him a fascinating assortment of perverts and, yes, black magicians. The skull and crossbones adorned the uniforms of the dread Gestapo. A double lightning bolt was the symbol of his Storm Troopers. Each man had it secretly tattooed out of sight under his armpit. (Rioters at the Democratic Convention in Chicago in 1968 were puzzled when the Chicago police forced them to strip to the waist and raise their arms so their armpits could be explored. Were the cops looking for SS agents?)

Hundreds of books about the Nazi movement have been written since World War II, many of them authored by intimates of Hitler and members of the Nazi inner circle. One recurrent theme in this literature is Hitler's mediumship and apparent demonic possession. His strange epileptic-type fits were classic manifestations of possession. Dr. Achille Delmas wrote, "A person close to Hitler told me that he wakes up in the night screaming and in convulsions. He calls for help and appears to be half paralyzed...He utters confused and unintelligible sounds, gasping, as if on the point of suffocation." Often when fully conscious, Hitler would suddenly cry out, "He is here! There! In the corner!" He would point to empty space, apparently seeing entities that no one else could see. Was it madness? Or was Adolf Hitler haunted by, even directed by, ultraterrestrials?

It is known that many men in Hitler's inner circle were members of the ancient Rosicrucian-style order *Thule,* a secret society that is supposed to have had its beginnings in Thule, Greenland, in ancient times. Himmler, Hess, and other prominent figures in the Nazi party spoke privately of strange goals: of creating a New Order in which the masses would be robotized to serve a select inner circle, who in turn would serve undefined supernatural forces. Dr. Joseph Goebbels, Hitler's brilliant minister of propaganda, won his Ph.D. with a thesis on *The Spiritual and Political Undercurrents of the Early Romantics.* In 1925 he wrote, "I want to be an apostle and a preacher." He became instead an apostle to the strangely mesmeric little ex-corporal who set out to rule the world. Like his boss, Goebbels had an incredible sense of history and the ability to sway the minds of large groups of people. Hitler, it is said, had such imposing presence and such a brilliant, decisive, seemingly logical mind that when generals and officials barged into his office prepared to argue with him about issues and decisions, they left cowed and awed, convinced he was the greatest man alive.

All kinds of kooks and cultists were welcomed into the Nazi inner circle. Many of them suffered from messiah complexes, convinced that Hitler was going to save the world rather than destroy it. Vidkun Abraham Quisling, the Norwegian traitor, is a minor but typical example. Quisling's father was a clergyman who had visited with angels and written books about them. In 1929, Quisling himself published *About the Matter That Inhabited Worlds Outside Ours and the Significance Caused by It to our Philosophy of Life.* Later he wrote another massive book called *Universismus,* which summarized his cosmology and outlined a new religion. He founded the Norwegian Nazi party in 1933 and served as premier during the German occupation of Norway, after virtually handing the country to Hitler on a platter. He was executed at the end of the war.

"After Quisling was imprisoned in 1945, he was convinced that he would have been able to reach the acme in all sections of art and science," Dr. G. Langfeldt wrote in the *Psychiatry Digest* in May 1970. "Of interest with respect to his paranoid ideas is that during the trial Quisling maintained on several occasions that he believed in a new world of God to come to this earth and that this faith had been the driving force in all his actions."

Quisling, like Hitler, was dominated by an overpowering sense of historical mission and, having failed in that mission, degenerated into a babbling lunatic.

European Gypsies were rounded up by the Nazis and slaughtered, as we have already noted. Hitler also maintained all-out war against scientists and philosophers who did not conform to his own beliefs and cosmology. Nazi gangs burned down the archives of Rudolf Steiner's Theosophical Society and attempted to wipe out his life's work. (Steiner was a major philosopher and student of the occult who made many outstanding contributions to human knowledge.) Books were wantonly destroyed, and the leading thinkers and intellectuals of Europe were either killed or driven into exile.

In his drive for world domination Hitler created a scientific establishment that developed new rocket weapons, revolutionary aircraft (such as jets), and worked toward atomic fission. The influence of this new science changed the world forever in the 1940s. One direct result was our voyage to the moon aboard craft designed by men trained in the laboratories of Nazi Germany.

In retrospect the Nazi era was a repetition of the earlier patterns of history. It is a pattern that will undoubtedly be repeated again, perhaps in the not-too-distant future.

One facet of Hitler's madness was demonic obsession with liquidating the Jews. Actually, his racism was much broader than anti-Semitism. To him *all* races were inferior to pure German stock. He sought to create a super-race that could run a worldwide government. And his fixation with the Jewish question was his urge to invalidate the ancient prophecies and thus alter the whole history of the future.

This brings us to the sticky and highly unscientific subject of prophecy. From the beginning, the ultraterrestrials have presented man with a fairly complete outline of his future and his destiny. On one level, millions of individuals have received precise predictions of future events in their own lives through mediums, oracles, and prophets who communicated with ultraterrestrials. On another level, every major culture has attempted to preserve their prophetic teachings by carving them in stone or sealing them in tombs and caves (as the Dead Sea Scrolls). All of these occult and religious records from all parts of the world offer essentially the same predictions. The Bible's Revelation of St. John is an outstanding example. It explains to us that the final war, Armageddon, will begin in the Middle East after the Jews have resettled in their ancient homeland. Obviously, if Hitler's evil crusade had succeeded, Israel would never have been created, and Armageddon would have been averted.

Nostradamus, a French physician in the sixteenth century, composed many verses that have since proved to be precise predictions of events that came centuries after his death (he even described the rise and fall of Napoleon). One of his most quoted prophecies is:

> The year 1999, seventh month,
> a great King of Terror will come from the skies,
> ...Around this time Mars to reign for the good cause.

Oriental armies will sweep across the world, according to many of these prophets. Even the Hopi Indians have a tradition that great hordes will invade North America from the Orient. The number 666 is stressed in the Bible and many other works. Invert it and you have 999. The Bible states repeatedly that all kinds of wonders will appear in the sky before the end comes. Man has been warned to be wary of false prophets and not to go into the desert to meet them. Scores of modern UFO contactees have had their encounters in remote desert areas.

All religions promise that the end of mankind will come suddenly, like the thief in the night. Some refer to this event as the Second Coming, the reappearance of Christ, the Harvest. The Hopis call it the Purification. To take the sting out of this threat—and the destruction of all humanity must be regarded as a threat—religious interpreters have presented it as a step upward towards the immortality of the individual soul. But if science is on the right track, if the soul is merely an extension of some giant energy field in the sky, then the process is more in line with the moon food concept of the Oriental philosophers. Withdrawal of these extensions or controls of the supermind of the cosmos would mean that the individual would be absorbed into it and cease to exist as a separate physical unit. Ego, personality, and memory, being properties of the physical body, would be left behind.

There are two fundamental forms of religion: (1) the worship of elementals and supernatural manifestations, already discussed; and (2) the awareness of and submission to the supermind of the cosmos. The Cosmic Consciousness. Buddhism is the best example of the latter. The former concentrates on worshiping manifestations, while the latter is devoted to understanding the whole.

We are witnessing a worldwide phenomenon today: mass illumination of millions of people, particularly young (under thirty) men and women in all walks of life. This process is quite well understood but never openly discussed in the mass media. In 1900 a Canadian psychiatrist, Dr. Maurice Bucke, published the first important study of the subject, *Cosmic Consciousness*. Illumination is basically a sudden, overwhelming insight into the whole structure of the cosmos and man's relationship to it. Suddenly, for a few brief seconds, the percipient understands everything with incredible clarity. In some cases the process occurs over a long period in the form of short flashes of insight that gradually add up. In others it takes place instantaneously with the percipient seemingly bathed in a reddish glow or caught in a beam of brilliant white light cast down from the skies (thus we have the ancient phrase, "He has seen the light").

No one is ever exactly the same after an illuminating experience. Mediocre men become great leaders, preachers, statesmen, scientists, poets, and writers overnight! Others divorce their spouses, quit their jobs, and embark on new careers that catapult them into unexpected prominence. Some fear for their sanity at first because the experience is so overwhelming. Some are unable to cope with it and disintegrate into various kinds of fanatics.

Illumination often accompanies UFO sightings, particularly when the witnesses are caught in a beam of light from the objects. Their IQ later sky-rockets, and their lives change appreciably. But as in all aspects of the general phenomenon, there seem to be other forces imitating this process and producing false illuminism. Young people experimenting with LSD and other hallucinogens sometimes have experiences that they believe are contacts with the Cosmic Consciousness but which ultimately prove to be destructive. Charles Manson is a good example of this. Some LSD users do, however, appear to undergo a pure form of illuminism, but it is likely that they were already illumination-prone and would have had the experience eventually anyway.

Psychic abilities appear to be hereditary, and this includes illumination. Many people attracted to metaphysics spend years of their lives following the secret teachings, meditating, and disciplining their minds in an effort to gain godhead (another term for mystical illumination). More often than not they only succeed in opening themselves up to possession and hallucinations similar to those incurred by the use of psychedelic drugs or the practice of black magic. Today's young people are rapidly gaining firsthand knowledge of the phantom world of demons and ultraterrestrials as a result of such efforts. The hippie underground newspapers and comic books were filled with a new lore of demons and demigods as well as much inside information on the cosmology of the supermind. Dr. Timothy Leary started the stampede to illumination and the Cosmic Consciousness in the late 1950s with his LSD experiments. Today the drug scene remains a very important part of the youth subculture, much to the alarm and confusion of the establishment.

The notorious music festival at Woodstock in the closing days of the 1960s was actually a mass illumination experience. The seemingly schizophrenic and destructive philosophy being touted by those young people was in fact identical to the program of the Illuminati three centuries before. A revolution of the mind took place almost unnoticed and certainly undeciphered by the older population and their establishment. There was a worldwide movement against violence and war (the cornerstone of civilization over these past several thousand years).

Another offshoot of the process was the rapid decline of organized religion. People who have attained direct personal contact with the Cosmic Consciousness (or who at least *believe* they have attained such contact) have no need for the rites and trappings of the old-time religions. There is no need to go to church when *your own head is your church.* The fear of death and the promise of immortality have always been one of the main appeals of all religions. But as Dr. Bucke noted in his study, one of the effects of illumination is the complete elimination of the death fear. The percipient suddenly understands with convincing clarity that he is merely part of the larger whole and that he is *assured* of immortality because his consciousness, the actuating mechanism of his physical body, survives as a part of the supermind. The Bible thumper's concept of heaven and hell is quite different from the illuminated's insight into the cosmic structure. This was not a movement toward atheism, as many horrified adults believed. According to the young people, it was instead a movement away from elementalism and the many misinterpretations the ultraterrestrial manifestations have inspired.

It seemed as if that, within a few years, many of our orthodox beliefs might seem as archaic and ridiculous as the belief in Zeus. This movement toward a higher truth had been predicted for a thousand years. In Catholic lore the last pope will be an apostate who will supervise the decline of the church. He will be named Peter, as was the first pope. The prophecy states that the final pope before Peter will be assassinated. In 1967 the Vatican removed the Throne of St. Peter from the basement, dusted it off, and put it on display for the first time in centuries.

The birth, life, and effect of Moses, Christ, and others were predicted well in advance. In these times we have been subjected to a new series of prophecies that extends beyond the earlier prophecies describing the days before Armageddon and the ultimate Harvest. Jeane Dixon and several other seers claimed that the anti-Christ was born somewhere in the Middle East on February 5, 1962. He would, they said, rise up and attract a huge following in the 1980s and would lead a large segment of humanity into the crisis-filled 1990s. There was a massive conjunction of planets on February 5, 1962, and Oriental astrologers caused considerable excitement with their claims that the world would come to end on that day.

Arthur C. Clarke, the British scientist, studied the UFO phenomenon in the early 1950s and summarized his findings in 1953 in the form of an astonishing novel, *Childhood's End*. He visualized the flying saucers as part of the psychic system of our environment, peopled by giant, winged beings remarkably similar to the strange Mothman allegedly seen by hundreds of people in the Ohio Valley during 1966–67.*

He described a last generation of children endowed with heightened psychic abilities and the total Cosmic Consciousness. While the Overlords silently watch from their flying saucers, this final generation suddenly merges into a single vast unit of energy and ascends to join the supermind of the cosmos. Their development is completed. They have reached the climactic stage of cosmic evolution—a form of intelligent energy that no longer needs the physical shell and all of its accouterments.

Close observers of the youth subculture of the sixties, from Dr. Leary to R. Buckminster Fuller, detected the tremulant beginnings of such a last generation among those born after 1945. As they came of age in the 1960s, a whole new cycle began. The Beatles really got the ball rolling with a cultural upheaval that is still continuing. Fantastic changes in political and occult belief occurred almost overnight. Anyone who read the daily newspapers could see that we are headed at breakneck speed into a new society with a whole new set of values. The decade of the 1970s was filled with violence and confusion as the restructuring took place on every level of society. The process was visible behind the Iron Curtain and in China also, and the Soviet Union eventually collapsed.

The year 1848 really marked the beginning of this massive collective overhaul of our planet. We now seem to be in the final stages of *something*— something of cosmic proportions. In order to play out the prophesied game,

---

*See *Strange Creatures from Time and Space* for many documented accounts.

the ultraterrestrials will need to create a new Hitler. The men who will confront him and hopefully defeat him were not too long ago sitting on floors in Greenwich Village, Paris, and Hong Kong, stoned on pot and tripping out on LSD. At least two American presidents, Abraham Lincoln and John F. Kennedy, showed all the signs of having undergone illumination. Winston Churchill and Charles de Gaulle were also likely candidates, as were Gandhi and possibly the late Gamal Nasser of Egypt. But there are no apparent Illuminati on the world scene at the moment. It is certain, though, that they will appear at the appropriate moment. They always have.

The sexual revolution is another key part of all this, for sexual repression and frustration have always been the basic cause of violence, peculiar social attitudes, and destructive psychoses. Fools that we are, we have always been in the habit of electing misfits to lead us—from Julius Caesar, who was an epileptic, to Adolf Hitler. Hitler's peers tried to crucify Sigmund Freud when he first dared to suggest this. But history demonstrates that he was right. We have followed an insane course for thousands of years. Once we took our finest young men to the top of a pyramid and cut out their hearts with pomp and ceremony. Today we send them off to battlefields. Once they happily climbed the pyramid under their own power. Now they are rebelling. They are questioning the system that wants their heart. The real hope of mankind may be that the system will break down or be drastically altered before our unknown Arab hears a voice in his head, dons a red cape, and gallops into the United States to free the Hopi Indians.

The members of WOW are still watching as they have always done, probably with considerable amusement. The ultraterrestrials are still running about in their black suits and a thousand other disguises, whispering in our ears, setting race against race and nation against nation. Our modern witch doctors, the scientists, are planting atomic bombs in known earthquake faults on the floor of the Pacific to see what will happen.

Great civilizations blossomed and died here before us. Others will certainly come after us, unless we leave the planet in such a polluted, radioactive state that it will be rendered unlivable for physical beings.

But even then we will have left our imprint behind. Thousands of years from now real visitors from some distant star may enter our solar system. They may stand upon our barren moon and look down at the burnt-out cinder that was once earth, and they may find a metal plate among the craters. It will puzzle their scientists because obviously the moon is uninhabitable and has never been settled. The plate will be just another erratic for their museum. They'll forget about it and never try to decipher the cryptic lettering. The lettering that states, "We came in peace for all mankind."

To order additional copies of this book,
please send full amount plus $4.00 for
postage and handling for the first book and
50¢ for each additional book.

Send orders to:

Galde Press, Inc.
PO Box 460
Lakeville, Minnesota 55044-0460

Credit card orders call 1–800–777–3454
Phone (612) 891–5991 • Fax (612) 891–6091
Visit our website at http://www.galdepress.com

Write for our free catalog.